Benoni, Immigrant Nurse and Educator

Bina Kulkarni

Thanks and Blessed

25/1/19

FBKMwando

Florence Benoni Kakunu Mwando

Fellow HE UK Academy, BSc(Hons) Health Care, RGN,
OND, DipHE, Cert Ed & Cert Community Eye Health

ISBN: 978-1-5272-2217-5

Cover & page design: Dean Murray, Eight Days a Week Print Solutions

Printed and bound by Eight Days a Week Print Solutions
Nottingham, United Kingdom

This book is dedicated to my father, Dryden
and my mother, Fonsiya.

Contents

Disclaimer

The contents, including photographs and images in this book follow my progression from childhood, to inexperienced nurse, to an effective professional Nurse Practitioner, Educator and traveler - as well as wife, mother and friend.

All places visited and worked at are factual. Images taken by the Nottingham University Hospital Trust (NUH) have been reproduced with permission from Neal Hughes. Statements from colleagues, friends and family have also been used with their permission.

Any technical or medical information included was current at the time I practiced. However, some nursing procedures described may have improved since my retirement because of updated technology and research.

This book is a personal account of my journey from Zambia to the United Kingdom (UK).

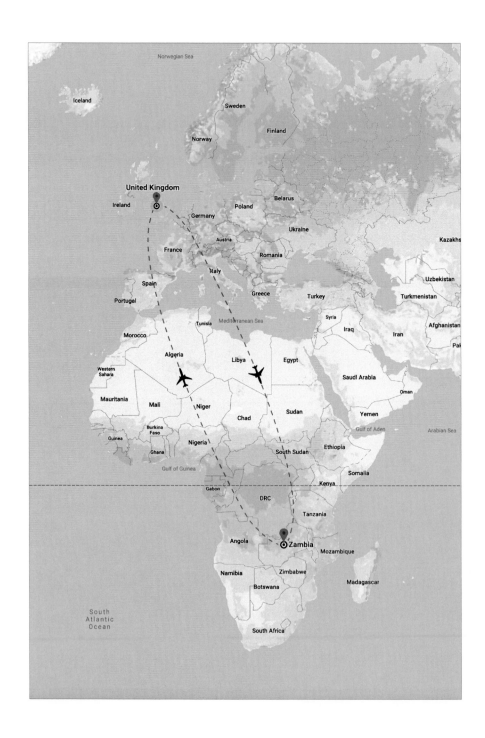

Foreword

The writing of this book is something I have wanted to do since 2003. During my nursing career I compiled student lesson plans, new staff induction and preceptor packs, and local and national presentations which led me to consider writing this book.

With encouragement from my father I travelled around different parts of Zambia and appreciated my good fortune in being able to do this. This is why it was so important for me to include my personal experiences. I have highlighted and acknowledged my late father, Dryden Stephen Samonu Yikona and his two brothers, Uncles Chimbundu Mpasela and Iyanvwa Konguboyi Yikona. My father was the youngest of three brothers. (Appendix 2 Yikona Family Tree).

My grandfather, Yikona Samonu Kazadi and his second wife Kamona Kanjenu had four children, my father being the youngest. I was named after the only girl, my Auntie Kakunu. My father was amongst the pioneers of medical assistant training, then based in Broken Hill (now called Kabwe), Zambia – which was then known as Northern Rhodesia.

After his graduation in 1944, my father was posted to Baluvale (now Zambezi) Hospital. Later he was moved by the Government to Lusaka

African Hospital (todays Lusaka University Teaching Hospital (UTH)). He had to move around because there was such a demand for people with his skills but they were few and far between.

From 1951-1954 Dryden was assigned to the Lilanda Hospital. He established a convalescent annex. This accommodated long-stay patients and those who travelled long distances.

Later my dad moved back to Lusaka African Hospital as the Head Medical Assistant.

From 1962-1964 he was posted to Mporokoso as District Medical Assistant which covered an area from Mporokoso to the shores of Lakes Tanganyika and Mweru wa Ntipa. This was just before Zambia gained its independence from Britain. During 1964-1966, my dad was then sent to Shiwang'andu, Chinsali and Mpika in the Northern Province. It was very hard for my mother and the children as we were constantly changing schools and languages.

Finally, from 1966 until his retirement in 1975, Dryden was in Broken Hill (Kabwe) working as a Provincial Medical Assistant for Central Province. He worked so hard performing his clinical duties; carrying out all the necessary administration and travelled constantly distributing medicines to local and peripheral clinics. At the same time he took great care of his family.

At the time there were no bakeries. My mum was very creative, making a hole in the ground, filling it with firewood and baking the bread in it. This is how I learnt to bake. My brothers would gather the firewood to heat the ground in preparation for cooking.

My dad's advice to us children and others was always to work hard, make education an important part of your life and always be honest.

I feel that I and all of my siblings grew up and obtained noble professions because of the influence of our dad's work and my mum and dad's sound parenting skills. We became medical doctors, teachers, lawyers, engineers and nurses, living life to the full and loving one another regardless of the physical distance or other differences between us. Both of our parents had great faith and every morning and evening we prayed together. Dad had a lot of missionary friends, including the late Pastor James Ford of Kabwe Chapel. Pastor James introduced me to missionaries when I came to the UK in 1979.

Dear dad, rest in peace. He was taken away from us on the 24th of August 1997.

"I miss you dad..." Below is the last letter my dad wrote to me in February 1997. It is in his usual memorable handwriting.

Date
5.3.97

Denkuku Farm
P.O. Box 16 0073,
Mwinilunga
Zambia.
C/Africa

Amyanani F.B.K. Mwando
Hayimushi wejima wenu.
Mudi nahi? Etu yetwawa tudi chiwahi.
China hohu. Kuzeya kwa mujimba, mulona
mujimba mafukisami anawuli dehi. 4old?
matelu ami kutiya china muntu ahoshi chakola
neyi choou. kutiya nehi. Sailas, Mantabe ni
samonu ni Ewa ni Mamboro adi nahi?

Iyanbwa ni nodindi adi nahi? photo ya
mwananu twatambwili tu nasakilili mwini.
Mafuku anahete mwijima neyisonekeleti dehi
nakwijileya kukala kudi hanu hafarm.
mulona anombi enda astwa ichi anatwi
dehi 32 natwiojoki akutwa nawa amakwawu.
anombi 31 hohu anashalwehu. Wushona wenu.
Mumulep Iyanbwa kanda 40 nenaku naka
mwoonekela nawa kwumbudi mulona postage
stamps. wuseya wenu. namusonekeli nawa
kaji kehu.

Nzambi ayihembi wejima wenu.
Mona   P.T.O.

6.3.97
Hatambuli makanda
neyi haloshi wejima
wetu ni mama yeyi
tu nasakilili chachewi
kutiya neyi mudi
chachiwahi. Ewa Suitcase
ichi dinu tukwenzulula.
mwakawy kwiyi twambi
katambula used clothes
yaku fumoku?
Nwala etu yidi na
kunoka nankashi
Day a night kunoka hohu
Nzambi ayikiswili wejima wenu.
Mona

vii

The Yikona Family

Our fathers, Iyanvwa Konguboyi, Chimbundu Mpasela and Dryden Samonu, were the sons of Kamona Kanjenu and Samonu Makala Yikona.

As previously mentioned, they had three boys and one girl. The girl, my Aunty Kakunu died early in life. The three brothers could best be described as 'three-in-one'. They loved each other for their whole lives up to the time of their departure from this world.

Iyanvwa and Mpasela never went to school and lived in a village. However, Dryden was educated and lived most of his life in towns. Because of the love that existed between the three brothers, the latter often wrote to his brothers to find out how they were doing. Iyanvwa also wrote often. This kept the spirit of unity amongst them. Added to this, every five years or so Dryden came to the village with his wife and family to visit.

Sometimes my parents would send the children home to meet my fathers' relatives. Other times dad would call one of his brothers to visit them in town. This spirit of unity that existed amongst the brothers was so strong that none of us children called my fathers' brothers 'uncle'. Instead we referred to both uncles as 'tata wa mukulumpi' (older father) or 'tata wa kansi' (younger father). Neither did we ever use the word 'cousin' but referred to our uncles children as brother or sister.

Our dads/the brothers were so close that when the eldest brother Iyanvwa, passed away his children were looked after by the two remaining brothers and treated as their own children.

A close bond remained between the two surviving brothers, and they encouraged all of us children, to do the same. This kept the family as one. Today our extended families try to keep up these strong bonds.

For this section I would like to acknowledge and thank my brother (cousin) Damson Yilun'a Nyamuyanda Yikona BA – ED (French/RE) deputy head Kasempa Boys, Headmaster Kabompo Boys, headmaster Mwinilunga Secondary, Headmaster Solwezi Technical and Principal Mwinilunga trades.

Introduction

In this book I have both researched and identified the meanings and origins of all my names; and reflected on my life as a nurse, wife and mother. It also describes my travels between Zambia and the UK.

Hopefully, it tells the story of the support I have both given and received from my family, friends and colleagues alike, and describes the established and worthwhile lifelong friendships I have acquired along the way with peoples of different and diverse tribes and cultures.

I have always had a willingness to learn and pass on my knowledge to others. This has enabled me to become a stronger person and to achieve a greater degree of responsibility in my career.

It has been a hard road to success but when you work hard and humble yourself the rewards can be abundant.

My faith in God has sustained me throughout both the good and hard times in my life. This has been especially comforting to me during bereavements; hardships and culture shocks, in particular when I arrived in the UK in winter from Zambia. However, when people ask me where I am from, I answer that, the same as everyone else I am from my mother's womb. This is not meant to be a facetious comment but we are all human and made in God's image. *'Behold, children are a heritage and gift from the Lord.'* Psalm 127:3.

The bible also says *'do unto others as you would have them do unto you.'* Matthew 7:12. Human beings in general and patients in particular, deserve the best of care. I believe that regardless of where one comes from or where one trained as a nurse, patients should always be treated the same and the focus of their care should revolve around their individual needs.

"Jesus said unto him, if thou canst believe, all things are possible to him that believeth" Mark 9:23.

Background

When immigrant nurses obtain a passport and work permit to work abroad, some of the indigenous nurses of that country question how an immigrant nurse can take one of their specialist posts.

The truth is there is no magic formula. It is not a mystery. The nurses' practice in terms of caring and utilising their clinical skills; their professional sound techniques that have been constantly practiced and a degree of talent beyond what is expected is in my experience how one can achieve these positions. Anyone, despite their background and ethnicity should strive to take advantage of equal opportunities.

This book is my journey but acknowledges legendary nurses who have been in a similar position to me. I describe what I feel I did well and my thought processes, showing what can be learnt. Some of my innovations can be put to use in other nursing practices.

I Benoni Florence Kakunu, known to everyone as Florence, originate from the Lunda Tribe in Zambia. I married Nelson, who is of the Tonga Tribe. Having been born and educated in Zambia, and obtaining scholarships from the British Council and Zambian Ministry of Health I came to the UK. In a foreign land, my identity took an additional dimension, that of belonging to 'an ethnic minority' group. However, I did not allow this to hold me back or bear a negative influence over me. Being optimistic at work and in life helped me build positive relationship with other immigrant nurses and indigenous nurses alike.

Now, as a mother of four children, a mother of my nephew, born in the UK, a grandmother of four - some of whom are of mixed parentage........ I feel that the cultural differences in my family are still important, however, we do not allow any negativity to arise from this. This is how I would like to see the rest of the world.

My eldest son is named after my late father-in-law Sailas Mwando. My eldest daughter is called Mantabe, meaning premature beer, which might not catch on in Britain! The elder sister to my late mother-in-law, Rebecca Ndambakuwa, was called Mantabe. My second son Samonu is named after dad, and my second daughter Evah is named after my late elder sister. My son (nephew) Mambwe is named after my brother-in-law (his father). As in some other cultures, we keep the family names from generation to generation.

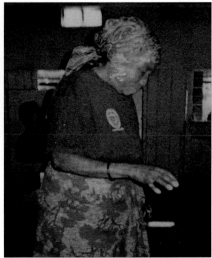

Father-in-law Sailas   Mother-in-law Rebecca Mwando

In our family, as in some other families, we can be described as truly international. Life in general can require the ability for us to have to relate to a greater diversity of people than ever before, and to work with people from other cultures different to one's own. My diverse familial background has helped strengthen my nursing development through being able to relate to persons of colour and creed.

My personal family situation and the passing on of my beliefs, has led to our younger generation accepting united families, despite coming from different backgrounds and cultures. Our family consists of peoples from all over the world including Africa, the European Continent, Asia, India and the new world countries. Indeed the world can be a small place. Older family members are regarded as natural mentors, our united family understands, forgives and tolerates one another.

I would like to point out that because this book is about my life as a nurse, and my father was in the same profession, the book concentrates mainly on my fathers' life as opposed to my mothers, but I loved them both equally and they were as important as each other to me.

Birth, Naming and Nursing Development

Left to right: Isaiah, Dryden, Abigail, Florence, Evah, Stanley, Lydia,
Fonisiya, Joel, Richard. (Joseph and Stuart were not born).

I was the fifth child and second eldest daughter from a family of ten children. I was born on the 6th July 1952 after a difficult labour. My mother named me Benoni, which comes from the Bible, Genesis chapter 35, verse 18. Florence was the midwife who delivered me. I was told that Kakunu was my aunt, the only sister to my dad, who my parents told me was very kind to others, whether she knew them or not. Yikona, my maiden name, is taken from the lakes of Mwinilunga (Lunda translation is Ijiya de Kona). My married surname Mwando means a string or rope. My late father-in-law was the head man of the Mwando Village.

My late father, Dryden Stephen Samonu Yikona, worked in the hospitals and clinics of Zambia. I often accompanied him because I was inquisitive and fond of his work. As I grew older, I spent my school holidays helping in the clinic. Despite infection control being a basic requirement in comparison to current policy, we were never infected.

My parents had big Government houses in Shiwanandu and Kabwe. There were always visitors staying with us, and most people thought my parents'

1

houses were like a bus stop which allowed transit visitors to be freely accommodated in the house, but we were more than happy about this. My brother actually described our house as being like a church but the children thought it was wonderful. These visitors included politicians, ministers and friends. My late father was amongst the first Principal Medical Assistants at The African Hospital which was in Northern Rhodesia, now University Teaching Hospital (UTH) in Zambia. From the exposure of my late father's hospital and clinic work, I was always named a matron or nurse by the visitors and friends who came to the house.

I grew up with a loving attitude and people knew me as the girl who was always laughing. Although I was under-age to be a carer, I was eager to look after anyone who didn't feel well, or who wanted to be fed or have a drink. Without seeking permission from my late mother I used to emulate her actions and 'nurse' people. Fonisiya Yihemba Samuwika (Yihemba in Lunda translated as carer), who was taken away from us in 2003.

My mother looked after her young sister, Edith, who always lived with us. Her daughter Catherine, my sister (technically cousin) has kindly sent this tribute to me for this book.

Tribute to Benoni Florence Kakunu Yikona-Mwando, our family Nightingale on the occasion of your book launch.

Florence is my sister going by the Lunda tradition. Our mothers were blood sisters. The late Mr. Dryden Yikona and Mrs. Yikona brought up my mother Mrs. Edith Ntemena Kabinda-Kadimba, from the age of four years until she was given in marriage to the late Mr. William Kawumba Kadimba. The love that existed between these families has left behind a lasting legacy. Now the wider families are so closely knitted together that the younger generation are not able to explain where the two branches first met.

Indeed, our family is amazing with well supported networks and our sister Florence has continued to play a key role in ensuring this legacy of love and care for one another, that was started by our parents, keeps burning from one generation to another. My hope is that writing a book such as this will keep our family history alive for years to come. Thanks for your support rendered to me and two of our children whilst they were studying in England. Thank you for organising family events. Now the next generation is also very close to each other. God bless you and our brother-in-law.

From **Mrs. Catherine Mulemba Pumulo Kadimba-Mwanamwambwa** MSc Poverty Reduction and Development Management, University of Birmingham UK, Public Administration and Economics, University of Zambia, Diploma in Education, Kwame Nkrumah University Kabwe, Zambia.

In 1972, the first ever thirteen Zambian doctors graduated from the University of Zambia. Among these doctors was my elder brother, the third born called Isaiah Yambeji Ernest Yikona. He encouraged me to join the Nursing School and supported me throughout my course with reassurance, and helped if any problems arose. In 1975 I graduated from Kitwe School of Nursing, Copper Belt Province, Zambia. Kitwe was partly run by immigrant and overseas nurse tutors. The overriding message they taught was that patient care is uppermost, and should be delivered in a professional manner at all times and under all circumstances. The Matron was a lady named Mrs. Evelyn (Namulwanda) Sanderson. Her husband was a white immigrant, which demonstrates the concept that immigration is a two-way process.

3

In Zambia, The General Nursing course I undertook was at diploma level, but it was a three year programme and equivalent to the UK degree. The official language used was English. To access this course 'A' level English, mathematics, general science or individual chemistry, physics, biology or physical science was required. There were also well established post-basic training programmes such as midwifery, mental health, nurse tutor training and research. Furthermore, ophthalmic care has recently been added as a post-basic programme at Chainama Hill. This is supported by doctors from the UK and the United States of America (USA) and includes lecturers from the University of Zambia.

In relation to nursing qualifications obtained in one country, these are sometimes accepted by other countries, but not in all cases. I had to do an adaptation course. Some skills are transferrable, as is a positive attitude, and I may be an independent nurse with freedom of autonomy but we all have to abide by rules.

"Though I am free and belong to no man, I make myself a slave to everyone to win as many as possible" 1st Corinthians 1:20-21.

My late eldest brother Stanley Yikona (taken away from us in 2013) worked for Shell and British Petroleum (BP) in Kitwe. His wife Mama Ya Lynn (also known as Nyampasa meaning the mother of twins) worked at Kitwe Central Hospital as a medical assistant. My late eldest sister Evah Kaluswika Kanombe was a secondary school headmistress at Mindolo Girl's School in Kitwe. This meant that my off-duty days and weekends when I was doing my nurse training were well spent at one house or the other. I always felt fully supported in everything by my whole family. I had no excuse to fail! I succeeded in gaining my nurse qualification in 1975 aged 23 years.

MR. STANLEY SANKENI YIKONA
ECCLESIATES 3: TO EVERYTHING THERE IS A SEASON

Thanks to the Zambian family of behalf of my late brother.

Qualified Nurse and Zambian Postings

In April 1975 I obtained my full registration from the General Nursing and Midwifery Council of Zambia to enable me to practice as a general nurse.

My first posting was to Mongu in Western Province to work at Lewanika District and General. Travelling by road from Lusaka to Mongu in 1975 took nearly ten hours, but by air I was able to arrive in just three hours. When I arrived in Mongu, I found there were three other nurses and myself sharing a four bedroomed house.

The hospital dealt with surgery; tropical and general medicine; obsetrics and gynaecology, ear nose and throat issues and eye problems. The hospital was not so developed as those in the UK. The patients were separated to some degree but the nurses were expected to look after all the different patient problems. We were also the cleaners, porters and to some degree clinicians. The psychiatric and infectious isolation wards, whilst on the same site, were located separately.

Ward settings were open and wide with spaced individual beds. The hospital had one Matron and one Medical Superintendent. A School of Nursing was incorporated in the hospital and a two-year Enrolled Nurse Training programme was available. Unlike today's hospitals, as a newly registered nurse I had no induction or supervision.

Most patients who came through spoke Lozi which is one of the seventy two dialects of Zambia. With no time to waste, I had to learn a few words in Lozi in order to communicate effectively as I could not rely solely on 'sign language' alone. The Mongu residents and patients called the new nurses immigrants (kimunyukunyuku fela, meaning foreigners) even though we were all from Zambia. Perhaps some things are universal.

I felt fortunate that the principal tutor during my nurse training - a Ugandan man who trained in the UK, taught me that to be a hospital nurse or university lecturer, (or indeed just a good human being) be professional and kind and you can develop priceless relationships with patients, learners, and colleagues. *"Failure will never overtake me if my determination to succeed is strong enough"* (Og Mandino).

In 1975 there was no digital observation equipment or technology to assist with assessments. In some ways nursing has not changed, accurate clinical sign and symptoms, any concerns or abnormalities need to be quickly referred to the senior nursing staff or medical colleagues. Documentation has to be filled in and recorded. We were also expected to know the patients' general conditions, specific diseases, and name and dates of birth without the use of wrist bands.

On my first day shift, there was a Russian doctor who was preparing a lady for a caesarean section. I had to go to theatre to assist as a scrub nurse with a sister who was an English nurse and theatre runner. My theoretical training as a student theatre nurse was sound, and putting it into practice assisting the obstetrician went very well. Both mother and baby were fine. I went home to my housemates feeling very happy. When they asked me why I was in such a good mood I told them I could not say because of patient confidentiality. A week later there was local news about the Russian doctor and the new staff nurse delivering the baby with a successful caesarean section. Perhaps I was over exuberant with my confidentiality issues!

Whilst living in the shared house, the four of us went shopping together by the riverside in Limulunga where we bought fresh fish, live chickens and bananas from the orchard. We all cooked and ate well. We laughed and shared jokes, and gave the tutors nicknames. One we named Jesus because he always wore sandles; pharmacopaea taught us pharmacology; glossina, ppd (protein purified derivative) depending on what lessons they taught. Like mnemonics it helped us remember. The nurse tutors did not know what we did, they were very strict. We had to be in our bedrooms by nine o'clock at night and Miss Farell always checked our bedrooms. I will never know how we succeeded in going out illegally to discos, and to agriculture shows, then study throughout the night to achieve high marks. The latter was a testament to our commitment to nursing. It is true that 'all work and no play makes Jack a dull boy'. Working and succeeding as a newly qualified registered nurse in Lewanika District Hospital in Mongu, meant having a strong will; special expertise; total commitment; dedication; resourcefulness; improvisation and resilience.

My first night shift, which was from 6.30pm - 7.30am, was hectic. The ward was full. There were forty patients with acute conditions and I had two student nurses with me. I also worked as a night superintendent, walking around the hospital with a night security guard checking all the wards. We had no electricity outside the building so I had to use a torch to inspect the premises.

Speaking little Lozi, I thought carefully about how to communicate with others, support those in need, and understand my limitations. As a newly qualified nurse who missed my parents' home, I had to remain focused and work well so that I could get paid and return to apply for a specialist nursing course. Six months passed quickly and it gave me a firm foundation in general registered nursing. Because I was able to cope with the circumstances I found myself in, I believed I could be an excellent nurse who could work as an 'immigrant'.

In September 1975 I was transferred to UTH in Lusaka. I had a special interest in ophthalmology, my elder brother had suggested I look at this option. My housemates specialised in midwifery. This hospital had recently been developed and upgraded, with more modern facilities and builds. This attracted new doctors, nurses and allied professionals - mainly from the UK, Ghana, Nigeria, Canada, Switzerland, USA, India and Zimbabwe.

In 1976 there were many nurses, doctors and railway professionals from Zimbabwe, Botswana and South Africa who practiced in Zambia. At the same time Zambian nurses and teachers were recruited to work in Mozambique. The first Zambian President, Doctor Kenneth Kaunda (in the late '70s to early '90s) set up refugee camps for some of the freedom fighters from Zimbabwe (at that time called Southern Rhodesia) and South Africa. Their leaders were regarded as comrades. They were fighting for independence from British rule. From the several countries mentioned, plus various Zambian dialects, it was a challenge to meet all the needs of the various nationalities due to the communication difficulties. We coped by complying with the nursing and educational Code of Practice that was laid down by the Zambian General Nursing and Midwifery Council, The Zambian Medical Council, Ministry of Health and the definitions outlined by the World Health Organisation.

"Life is 10% what happens to you and 90% how you react to it" (Charles R Swindoll)

In October 1975 I was accommodated in a nurses' hostel in a single room with shared communal toilets, bathrooms, sitting room and kitchen. We were allowed to have either a one or two plate cooker within the single room as long as we were responsible and fulfilled the Health and Safety Act 1974. I had a few pots, cutlery, plates and tea cups.

I started working on a general medical/surgical ward as a general registered nurse. This ward had a few side rooms and a wide sister's office with a long glass window facing the main ward. The other side of the ward had a nice view to the outside. It was on C floor, opposite was the orthopaedic and gynaecology wards. The sister knew immediately if we failed to do a proper hospital corner on a bed!

Towards the beginning of 1976, I discovered the Zambian Committee for the Prevention of Blindness, which was based in Ndola in the Copper Belt. I knew Ndola Central Hospital because I had attended there for six weeks of a psychiatry placement whilst a student nurse in 1973. Dr. Kwendakwema who had trained in Russia went to Ndola and together with Dr. Chelemu were running peripheral ophthalmic work with the Zambian Flying Services. I was invited there to learn about what services they were providing. I became heavily involved as a committee member. This led to further opportunities in a corporate position in 1989 (as discussed later) with the support of Helen Keller.

By 1976 the medical/surgical ward was moved to E and G block. Ward C12 became the Maxillofacial, Ear, Nose, Throat and Eye ward, where I became a senior staff nurse. There was only one Ophthalmic Consultant, Dr. Shukla, who originally came from India. As a university teaching hospital, it had everything I needed to develop as an experienced general and ophthalmic nurse. The hospital provided advanced training from specialist health professionals, thus creating an opportunity to progress.

In 1976 I decided to request my transcripts i.e. all of my recorded training. This is required if a nurse wishes to work abroad. It is a complicated, time consuming and expensive process. It involved obtaining records of all my training and education - how many hours I worked in the educative process of nurse training; comments in regard to my performances, character etc. It meant getting in touch with various specific people. In my case for example, these were:

- Mr. Zzizinga, our principal tutor
- Registrar Mrs. Ruth Banda, of the General Nursing and Midwifery Council of Zambia
- Individuals such as Dr. Shukla,
- The Registrar of the United Kingdom Nursing and Midwifery Council

It is sometimes not easy to achieve this. I was thankful that all parties involved supported and recommended my application and approved it.

In fact Dr. Shukla stated that upon returning from further studies, Florence would be an asset to the eye ward as well as the Lusaka University Teaching Hospital.

I applied for and was successful in obtaining a British Council Scholarship. The process of getting an external scholarship award took a long time from its inception in Zambia to acceptance in Scotland at the Royal Infirmary of Edinburgh.

In January 1979 I received news that I had to report to the Cabinet Office, where study grants were approved and signed off. I was scared but decided to be brave because although I was apprehensive about my scholarship application being turned down, I was still grateful I had a job. Whilst I was in the office we heard several bombs go off as attempts were made to assassinate some of the fighting leaders from Southern Rhodesia in nearby refugee camps. I was informed that my application had been successful but I immediately said that I would return later and deal with it because my concern was getting back to the hospital. The situation meant dealing with different types and numbers of injuries and I had to very quickly become efficient in screening and selecting those with life-threatening conditions and referring them to senior nursing staff/medical colleagues. This practice carries on in today's healthcare systems in A&E departments and is known as triage.

I went to see the Assistant Chief Nursing Officer a few days later at the Ministry of Health, and was congratulated before I had time to even enter. Miss Kasapo said "Well done mwaice" (mwaice is Bemba meaning young) Nurse Yikona and advised me to go the British Council Office immediately for interviews and briefings.

Halpern and Cheung (2008) wrote a book entitled 'Women at the Top' about powerful female characters that could show other women how to successfully combine work and family. It describes some actual women and their lives; one of these was called Rita. A quote from Rita's factual family life said "my family is priority number one. I must have a reasonably happy family before I can serve the public. Family has always been a safe harbour for me, especially when I face a lot of pressures outside". Similarly to Rita, I ensured the safety and well-being of my family before taking the necessary steps to move abroad and become an immigrant nurse and educator even though this was twenty nine years previous to this publication. On reflection I feel that all my life I may have been ahead of the pack!

I went to inform the Senior Matron, Rosemary Mumba, and Dr. Shukla that I was going to Edinburgh, Scotland in the UK. My parents were in Kabwe, far away from Lusaka. There were no mobile phones to text, or computers to email the good news so I travelled home to tell them. I was very lucky because I arrived home alive, I survived the Zambian minibus and roads. It took some time, as unlike in England, minibuses do not leave until all the seats and aisles are full. However, some of the time was made up by the way they drove. My parents were very kind Christians and I knew that upon arrival we would all sit down and give thanks to God for the continued blessings. My father drove to Mr. James Ford, who was in charge of the Christian Mission in 'Many Lands Church', in Kabwe and with great joy, shared the good news.

I had to have vigorous and thorough medical examinations and vaccinations prior to entering the UK. Paid study leave forms were checked and approved before the air ticket was issued. Travel and tourism are major components of education in Zambia.

With the two weeks of preparation I had before I travelled to the UK, I tried to learn about different aspects of British society by attending lectures and tutorials supplied by the British Council. I read about Florence Nightingale (and later Mary Seacole) who were the first nurses to be involved in caring for the injured during the Crimean War. I explored in detail Florences' nursing history and felt I could relate to this nurse named Florence. Anionwu (2005) in her book about the life of Mary Seacole, mentioned a person named Elizabeth Purcell who was an 'almost black' nurse described as an 'exemplary character' but who was unable to go to the Crimea - she was rejected because of her age (fifty-two) and colour. This was not going to happen to me and many others around the world.

I come from a diverse nation, which has over seventy two dialects, so learning and understanding different cultures helped me to adapt in the UK.

Post Basic Training in UK

I flew to England in January 1979 where I was met by a British Council representative. It was snowing interspersed with heavy rain. I was wearing a traditional Zambian chitenge with sandals that were so beautiful. This was a total culture weather shock. I was cold and shivering. Dr. Neil Nkanza, a Zambian man who was training to be a pathologist, immediately came to my rescue and took me to his wife Mary, also a nurse. We spent the afternoon shopping and I bought a winter coat and boots. I obviously needed more than two week's preparation for the weather!

It was the1970's and there was a winter of discontent. The Conservatives had been voted into power and the government was led by Margaret Thatcher. There was tension amongst a lot of workers, including healthcare professionals, and some of them were on strike when I arrived. I found this absolutely incredible as it would not have even been thought of in Zambia. I was shocked to find myself in such a situation where members of the armed forces were carrying rubbish bins because of striking bin men. In fact I thought 'Oh my goodness, at home they told me it was a 'green and pleasant land'!

I was taken to King's Cross station to catch a train to Edinburgh Waverley Station. To my amazement, I could not believe how many trains and platforms there were. In Zambia we had only one railway line, one passenger train, and a few trains transporting goods and minerals from the mines. Another British Council guide met me and seemed very excited to meet me. I was very relieved to see him as they did not appear to be on strike in Scotland! We went to the nurses' home at the Royal Infirmary. The nurses' home was called 'Florence Nightingale'. I took this as another good sign. The following day I toured the hospital and saw the different departments, including the laboratory where Alexander Fleming discovered penicillin. I found this very exciting, I had learnt about Mr. Fleming and the history of antibiotics when I was a student nurse in 1973.

The Principal Nursing Officer, Barbara Snowden, showed me the Princess Alexandra Eye Pavilion where the Eye Care Centre was based, together with the School of Nursing. I would have to be successful in The Adaptation course to be able to register with the Nursing and Midwifery Council in the

UK as a Registered General Nurse. After this I would then be able to proceed as a post basic student nurse in ophthalmology. This is what happened; in fact I passed the adaptation in seven weeks whereas some people took up to six months. I also gained my Scottish Badge. I was helped by my previous experience in Zambia, plus I was extremely determined to succeed.

The British Council paid my registration to practice in Scotland, it cost three pounds and fifty pence every three years.

I was given seven uniform dresses, aprons, head caps, belts and a badge. I was wearing one of the Zambian Kitwe School of Nursing badges and when walking down a corridor one of the clinical instructors, Mrs. Thompson, who had previously worked at this school, recognised my badge. We were very excited to meet one another.

When I was working on the ophthalmic wards one person in particular became an important part of my nursing life and my whole life. Margaret Studley was a ward sister but she had started training as a clinical instructor two days a week. She was an excellent role model and mentor. She was supportive and considerate. Mrs. Studley's guidance and instruction helped me into my successful life as an immigrant nurse and mother of a united family because of the beautiful way she treated me. At weekends she would sometimes take me shopping around Edinburgh or to some of the tourist sights. This was in her own time.

By April 1979 I was busy with the ophthalmic nursing course. The course consisted of both theory and practical work. The teaching was taught by senior doctors; nurses and visiting lecturers from their specialist areas. The course was based on the national curriculum. There were twelve of us in the class, six registered nurses and six enrolled nurses. It was such a small class, and of a more intimate nature, it promoted a greater teaching/learning environment. This benefited me greatly. I feel I might have struggled in a much large classroom setting.

The course lasted six months. The standard of teaching was extremely good so I felt I had no excuse to fail. I was also aware that being sponsored put me under some self-imposed pressure. As a sponsored student I wanted to achieve the best possible results to encourage further sponsoring of other nurses on my return to Zambia.

On the wards both the senior nursing staff and tutors were very strict. All the nursing duties that were required to be carried out were expected to be of the highest standard and constant monitoring took place.

The hospital examinations took place in October. The examination strategy for the Ophthalmic Nursing Diploma comprised of a nationally set written examination of pathophysiology and nursing knowledge. Clinical ability was examined by external assessors. The process involved an oral viva and the completion of selected skill procedures such as assembling instruments for minor operations. One doctor asked me about the side effects of steroid eye drops and in retrospect I gave a very accurate and comprehensive answer, although at the time I thought I might have failed. This was obviously not the case as I was awarded both the Ophthalmic Badge and the NMC for Scotland Badge. By Christmas 1979 I went back to Zambia very proud of my ophthalmic qualifications.

The Royal Infirmary of Edinburgh
Princess Alexandra's Eye Pavilion

This is to Certify that

Florence Benoni Yikona

followed a Course of Instruction in

Ophthalmic Nursing

from 2·4·79 to 1·10·79
and completed the practical and theoretical
requirements, giving satisfaction in the
Hospital Examinations.

7. 11. 79
Date

J. S. Robertson
Divisional Nursing Officer.

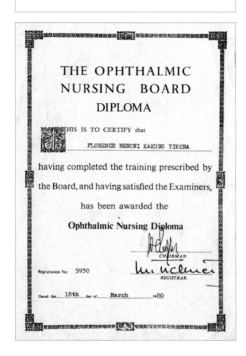

THE OPHTHALMIC
NURSING BOARD
DIPLOMA

THIS IS TO CERTIFY that

FLORENCE BENONI KAKUMU YIKONA

having completed the training prescribed by

the Board, and having satisfied the Examiners,

has been awarded the

Ophthalmic Nursing Diploma

CHAIRMAN.

REGISTRAR.

Registration No. 5930

Dated this 18th day of March 1980

Senior Staff Nurse and Mulungushi Supervisory Course

Back home in Zambia I commenced work in the Ear, Nose, Throat and Eye ward, UTH in Lusaka. This was in January 1981. I undertook in-house training as part of the preparations for nursing development which included career advancement. It was a precursor to becoming a ward sister as it gave experience in management training.

In 1982 I went to the Presidents Citizenship College, Mulungushi in Kabwe and obtained the Supervisory Management Course certificate for Nursing Personnel. The course covered all aspects of supervisory management including the psychology and the political aspects of it. It provided me with a good foundation for becoming a Sister which I then achieved. I was allocated ward C12 which consisted of a mixture of ear, nose, throat and eye patients plus aspects of maxillofacial surgery.

PRESIDENT'S CITIZENSHIP COLLEGE

Industrial Relations Unit

Final Results for Supervisory Management for Nursing Personnel

Duration:.... Three Months.........................

Name:.... Florence Benoni Kakuñu Yikoña Mwando.......

Subject	Result
	C+
Supervisory Management	
Psychology	C
Industrial Relations	C+
Field Project	C+
Sociology	B
Labour Economics	B
Political Education	B

KEY TO GRADES

A+	-	90% plus	- Distinction
A	-	80-89%	- Distinction
B+	-	70-79	- Meritorious Pass
B	-	60-69%	- Very satisfactory
C+	-	50-59%	- Definite Pass
C	-	40-49%	- Bare Pass
D+	-	30-39%	- Bare Fail
D	-	20-29%	- Definite Fail
E	-	Less than 20%	- Worthless

Date: 27th May 1982

Course Coordinator's Signature

EJS/gnm:
26:5:82

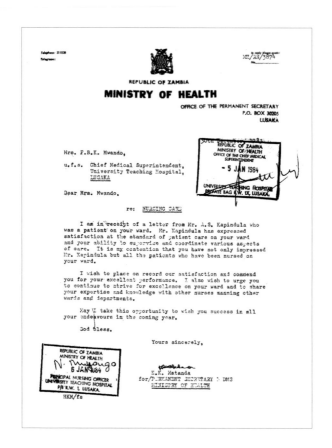

I immediately got involved in teaching colleagues and students in both clinical areas and the School of Nursing. My personal belief is that if people are able to progress and have the opportunity, they have a duty to do so. I performed my work to the best of my ability and to the highest standard I was able to achieve. I extended my work into the ophthalmic theatres and clinics under the guidance of Dr. La and later, Dr. Shukla. I imparted any new found knowledge to colleagues.

By April 1983 I was also involved with the mobile eye clinics. For these we travelled to Mazabuka. It was two hours away by road because of the state of the roads and we were carrying delicate instruments so drove carefully to avoid pot holes. I assisted the doctor in carrying out major eye operations, but performed minor ones myself. We had an eye clinic and left eye preparations that were necessary until our next visit.

Whilst working in the School of Nursing, I met Catherine Kalinda and Hilda Kaunda who had both trained in Wales as Nurse Tutors. They both advised me to apply and undertake a general nursing teaching course in Cardiff as I was already doing some teaching and this would benefit me greatly, which in turn would do the same for students. As a result of this I started to establish close contact with the University College, Cardiff. I also made contact with Moorfields Eye Hospital in London as this would provide me with an attachment placement for specialised ophthalmology teaching. I applied again to the British Council, through the Ministry of Health, for a scholarship. It is a department in the Ministry of Health that makes the recommendation to the British Council to award the scholarship. I was successful. It helped that the Chief Nursing Officer, Helen Matanda, on behalf of the Ministry of Health, sent a letter regarding my excellent performance in relation to the high standard of care given by me.

By this time I was married to Nelson Mwando. The rules in both Britain and Zambia stated that a married woman had to have permission from her husband before the British Scholarship could be awarded. Nelson had to sign to say he approved the application. When I moved to the UK to take up this scholarship Nelson remained in Zambia to look after our children.

I have not included any details of how Nelson and I met, I have left this for my romantic husband to describe, which he does so in Appendix 1.

L-R: Sailas, Florence, Samonu, Nelson, Lydia

Nurse Tutor Training – Retford and Cardiff

In May 1984 I was awarded the scholarship and prepared to study in England and Wales. A representative from the British Council walked with me to the Bank of Zambia to obtain approval of the foreign exchange currency. Mr. Ernest Phiri assisted me in processing the money on time.

I arrived at Moorfield's Eye Hospital and was met by the Director of Nurse Education and the Ophthalmic Board, Brenda O'Callaghan. They organised my placement orientation programme and I was so happy to be in one of the biggest hospitals in the world to specialise in ophthalmology. I was introduced to Tim Ossei, Lynne Bates and Ramesh Seewoodhary, all staff within the School of Nursing.

'Eton Hall International in Retford

My teaching course started in September, so my early arrival allowed me to familiarise myself with the wards and observe the different nurse tutors and clinical instructors in their preparation of clinical sessions and teaching plans for their specific and general subjects.

From 16th July - 11th August 1984, I was one of the overseas nurses who were sent to Eton Hall International in Retford, Nottinghamshire, in order to prepare themselves for entry to Cardiff University. The subjects included British history and culture, all aspects of communication – both verbal and written and the nursing curriculum. I learnt a lot from mixing with colleagues from Trinidad, Swaziland, Lesotho and India. There were differences between us but we co-operated in harmony.

On the 9th September 1984 I reported to the University Accommodation Halls in Cardiff. This was where all the theory took place with travel to London for the practical sessions.

I was amazed to see some of the indigenous students arrive in fancy cars. Of course I later realised this was normal for working adults, but it reflects my background from a developing country.

The day after I arrived, I met Mr. Colin Mutton, the head tutor in the Department of Education. The course included all aspects of the requirements for the methods of general adult teaching, covering all associated subjects plus your own specialty, which in my case was ophthalmology. We learnt about the use of visual aids; the need for the correct teaching materials and how to carry out research and critical analysis. We were also taught the importance of having fun as this helps students remember what they are taught. Flexibility was key.

Life membership letter

Some of my colleagues were impressed with my public speaking abilities and the knowledge I demonstrated in discussions and seminars. My teaching practice was mainly at Moorfields Hospital where I taught different professionals. I also taught at Newham General Hospital.

Upon completion I joined the International Ophthalmic Nurses Association (IONA) as a life member.

During my teaching practice I was at the Institute of Ophthalmology where Professor Barrie Jones was leading community eye health. He was very interested in one of my previous presentations and this resulted in him applying for a six-month extension of my scholarship to run from July - December 1985. Mr. Mutton called me to confirm that I had been awarded an extended scholarship to study Community Eye Health at the Institute of Ophthalmology - which was the associate of Moorfields Eye Hospital. So for this period I remained in London. I jumped for joy at this news and Mr. Mutton shook my hand and encouraged me to be prepared for more hard work. This course was for doctors so I and another nurse were the first two to access it. I felt it was incredible that someone from my background (and the first Zambian nurse) could be here doing this together with these medics and a Chief Nurse.

Community Eye Health Training in Ophthalmology – London

From July 1985 I commenced the Community Eye Health course under the direction of Professor Barrie Jones. Other lecturers included Dr. Jock Anderson, Dr. Allen Foster and Angela Reid. Dr. Anderson was very kind and made us all feel at home. Dr. Foster previously taught in Tanzania. He is now a Professor at the London School of Hygiene, heading ophthalmology. Angela Reid taught Economics.

The course was excellent and covered an amazing amount of eye-related topics ranging from the causes and complications of diseases to levels of eye health services in primary, secondary, tertiary and mobile care. But also covered more general subjects such as epidemiology and statistics and designing leaflets. Stressed throughout the course was to meet the target of 'Vision for All' by 2020. There were continuous assessments, projects and examinations, both written and practical.

In November 1985 I obtained a certificate in Nurse Tutor and Community Eye Health training from the British Government as part of its Technical Co-operation Programme, endorsed by the Minister of State for Foreign and Commonwealth Affairs, and Minister for Overseas Development.

This is to certify that

FLORENCE BENONI KAKUNU MWANDO

completed a course of instruction in

NURSE TUTOR TRAINING
and COMMUNITY EYE HEALTH

from   MAY 1984   to   NOVEMBER 1985

provided by the British Government

as part of its Technical Co-operation

Programme.

MINISTER OF STATE FOR FOREIGN
AND COMMONWEALTH AFFAIRS
Date 1.11.85   AND MINISTER FOR OVERSEAS DEVELOPMENT

Back to Zambia

I returned home to Zambia in 1986 where I worked full-time in the School of Nursing at UTH for one year before my teaching qualification was verified and I was registered as a Nurse Tutor. It was important I returned to the hospital, as promised, because it was to fulfil the requirements of the scholarship. Any deviation from this could have jeopardised future students in the same position. Mrs. Mercy Mbewe was the Principal Tutor. Other tutors included Mrs. Kate Chintu, Hilda Kaunda, Catherine Kalinda, Sarah Nsofu, Mary Mulwila and Mrs. Mary Sichinga Tembo and her friend Mercy Chikoti. All worked closely and faithfully demonstrated the values and qualifications of professional nurse tutors.

Between 1986 and 1989 I became one of the tutors in the University Department. I taught anatomy and physiology; the principles of general and surgical nursing and ophthalmology. I used the study skills and styles learnt at Eaton Hall in the UK. I encouraged student nurses to carry a note book at all times in order to take any important notes.

I was involved with the assessments and selection of applicants into The School of Nursing. The criteria were strict. Heavy make-up, bright nail varnish and jewelry were not suitable or encouraged. Nursing is a difficult profession which requires commitment and bravery. Not everybody has the capacity to deal with bodily fluids and end of life care.

In 1988 an ophthalmic laser machine was installed in the eye clinic (Clinic 7) at UTH. At this time I was working full-time in the School. Dr. Shukla and Dr. Anne Walters in the clinical area were both in discussion with Mrs. Mary Chibungo Zyongwe (the main principal of the School of Nursing) as the doctors stated that they needed me to work with them in the eye clinic. I was the only trained ophthalmic nurse. Eventually Mrs. Zyongwe agreed to this after I promised I would continue with some work in the school.

I was a passionate ophthalmic worker. I was happy to have care-giving responsibilities. I also became an expert at multi-tasking. Mr. Kaputula, also worked in the clinic as a clinical officer (these officers performed certain medical and nursing duties) and had an interest in eye care in both the primary and tertiary setting. This is how we ended up being involved in the mobile clinics together. Minor operations in the clinic were carried out by Mr. Kaputula and myself.

Dr. Shukla and Dr. Anne Walters – who is now in Fyfe, Scotland - had long waiting lists and increasing pressure from the growing population in Lusaka and its peripheral centres. Mr. Kaputula and I were trained in treating and giving accurate advice to patients, this then helped to reduce the waiting times, which in turn meant the doctors could spend their time performing major eye operations.

In loyalty *"I no longer call you slaves, because a master does not confide in his slaves. Now you are my friends, since I have told you everything the Father told me"* John 15:15

We continued our education through the doctors teaching us informally whilst practicing. Added to this, from 1988 The Journal of Community Eye Health was published, headed by Dr. Murray McGavin. Two years later the International Resource Centre was established. Both of these were excellent sources of information.

The complicated and heavy ophthalmic workload meant less hours at home, even so I continued to take students' work home to be marked. My husband Nelson worked long and hard too. He was an electrician at The Zambia Electricity Supply Co-Operation (ZESCo) and also came home late and tired. Several family members - including cousins; nieces and my sister-in-law helped at home with cleaning, cooking and looking after our children. We would all sit and eat together. Although we had different schedules, family support and mutual guidance, as and when needed kept us happy.

My husband has always been an incredible, helpful and understanding person. Nelson has always taken responsibility for the maintenance of home equipment such as the cooker, drain pipes, sinks and clock settings. He would also pick me up from work and the children from school, but would send a driver if he was stuck at work. Nelson's personality and love for the family has contributed to the united family. My late parents and in-laws all believed in him and trusted him. My cousins and friends used to say that there was always plenty of food and relaxation in our house and good music and jokes. As a wife, I have always appreciated it.

In 2002 Nelson took annual leave to fly from Nottingham to Zambia. He hired a car, driving for two days from Lusaka to Mwinilunga and back, just to see my mother, older brother Stanley, Damson and Mrs Kadochi (Stanley's mother-in-law). The love he shows, not only for me but my family members and friends, is amazing. Nelson, like love is amazing. Love breaks all barriers including distance - even Whatsapp cannot beat it.

On this trip Nelson got moved to business class on the aeroplane and ended up sitting next to the wonderful Kenneth Kaunda, our ex-president who united the country. Because of him we became 'One Zambia, One Nation'. This was a highlight in Nelson's life as they got to shake hands.

HELEN KELLER INTERNATIONAL INCORPORATED

VIT⊙P
VITAMIN A TECHNICAL
ASSISTANCE PROGRAM

November 6, 1990

Ref: 11/90-07

Ms. Florence Mwando
Community Eye Health
Univeristy Teaching Hospital/Nursing School
P. O. Box 50001/Eye Clinic
Lusaka, Zambia

Dear Ms. Mwando:

Enclosed please find a copy of the proceedings of the East, Central, and Southern African Regional Workshop on Vitamin A Interventions and Child Survival. After several months of collecting papers and editing, we are happy to bring you a finished document and hope you will find it to be a valuable reference tool and remembrance of your participation in the workshop.

Unfortunately the group picture taken at the workshop did not turn out. We are trying to trace the photo taken by the Zambian Ministry of Health but have not yet succeeded in getting a copy. If we receive a group photo, we will make copies and send them to all participants.

Thank you for your participation in the workshop. We hope it was a worthwhile experience that is continuing to have an impact on your work.

Best wishes,

Nancy Haselow/Diana DuBois
Technical Assistance Unit
Vitamin A Technical Assistance Program
HKI/NY

NH:jm

75TH ANNIVERSARY...WORKING MIRACLES SINCE 1915
15 WEST 16TH STREET NEW YORK, NY 10011 PHONE: 212-807-5800 TELEX: 668152 FAX: 212-463-9341

In 1989 we had an East, Central and Southern African Regional Workshop in Lusaka on the subject of vitamin A intervention and child survival. The people involved included the Government departments of Health, Education and Agriculture. Helen Keller's Corporation and the Ministry of Health worked together to bring this workshop about. I took an active role in this workshop, so much so that The Helen Keller International Corporation in the USA asked me to work with them. I declined as I did not want to go through the whole process of applying for visas and studying to live in a different country again. Besides this I was more than happy with my present position and life.

Back to UK

In 1990 I returned to the UK to attend an International Ophthalmic Nurses Association (I.O.N.A.) Conference, at their invitation. During this time, I also visited my late sister and brother-in-law, Abigail and Humphrey Chintu, and their son Mambwe in Cardiff, Wales. His father Humphrey Chintu was in the process of finishing his studies, and after this planned to go back home to Zambia.

It was at this time I started to think about living in the UK. I applied for a job in the Nottingham Eye Department following an advert in The Nursing Times. Mrs. Joan Hamilton, then Matron, and Sister Ann Watts of eye ward B47 interviewed me. Following my successful interview I remember Mrs. Hamilton telling me, as she took me to the sewing room for uniform measurements, not to let her down. This was great advice, it motivated me to work hard. I received a letter from Human Resources informing me that I had to contact Ann Watts immediately, as I had been given a four year work permit from the Home Office dated 9th August. A week later Dr. Edwards, the Chief Executive, welcomed me in a letter and asked me to report for work.

I had a Christian welcome from Pastor David Beresford of the Oasis Christian Centre in Beeston. He was amazing and his welcome put me at ease in Nottingham. To this day I still attend. The present pastor Nigel Yates performed Evah's baptism and Lydia's wedding. It also gave me the opportunity to meet more immigrants who later became friends. These included two Zambians, Doris Bradshaw and Patricia Kirk, whose British husbands worked in Zambia before they returned to the UK. They were such an important part of my children's lives.

Initially I was given temporary accommodation in the Hospital Residential Block. This was a room with shared facilities. I started working as a staff nurse in the eye clinic. In January 1992, I moved into one of their two-bedroom flats in preparation for my family coming to join me in February. The rent for this flat was reasonable and included all the bills except for phone calls. My sons Sailas and Samonu, and daughters Lydia and Evah arrived with their father. We did not have a repeat of the snow and rain incident as this time I was much better prepared - with coats!

On 5th April 1993 we moved to a council house. The Pastor came and prayed in the house for blessings. I paid rent every two weeks to the Nottingham City Council. The home warden kindly gave us a few pots, a small black and white television and a chair. Ann Watts was also very kind and caring towards my family, we felt she was almost a family member. Later In the month Ann and her partner Ben, brought us a large white fridge, dining chairs and material which Nelson used to upholster the seat cushions. We used the fridge for more than three years until we bought a new one. Nelson and Sailas bought a second-hand cooker, cleaned and repaired it, then connected it. The cooker lasted for four years before we had to replace it. We were surrounded by very kind people.

Mr. Colin Harper and his wife Ann, who worked in Zambia for many years, recognised me when they attended the eye clinic. Colin Harper knew my parents from church work in Kabwe. The following day, he returned with gifts of warm clothes and blankets.

As a new employee working with patients, I had an Occupational Health screening and medical vaccinations. I worked Monday to Friday 8am to 5pm. I had an induction programme. Corinna Maltby from the School of Nursing and one of the senior nurses from the eye ward, Sue Ashby, taught us. I met the Ophthalmic Clinical Director, Mr. Stephen Howarth, who told me he had a relative who worked in Zambia in the Copperbelt. This initial chat with him helped to put me at ease.

There were five consultants when I started working in the ophthalmology department. The nursing staff consisted of one matron, three sisters and two charge nurses. These covered the eye wards, clinic, casualty and theatre.

In 1992 it was decided to hold fellowship exams at the Queen's Medical Centre (QMC). Following this, in July, I received a letter from the Royal College of Ophthalmologists - sent by the Examinations Officer Elizabeth Hunt, to thank us (Kathy Neoh and myself) for helping organise the flow of examiners, fellowship doctors and the patients through their practical examinations.

I attended an I.O.N.A. Conference at Grey College, University of Durham, which was a three-day event taking place in April 1993. It was an innovative conference. I learnt of the different ophthalmic units worldwide and how common ophthalmic conditions were managed. It was also a great opportunity to network and socialise with other professionals.

Bereavements and Nottingham Trent Course

On 31st March 1994, I lost my younger brother, the eighth born, Joel Mwabi Yikona. He worked for the Bank of Zambia as an Economist. He was a Graduate from the University of Zambia and was scheduled to come to Wales for further studies in April, but a week before this he became ill and passed away. It was a difficult period for me but with the support I received from Queen's Medical Centre staff and Pastor David Beresford of the Oasis Christian Centre, I pulled through.

In October 1994 I applied to Nottingham Trent University to study for a Diploma in Higher Education and Health Studies. The Queen's Medical Centre sponsored my studies as well as granting me study leave. Unfortunately, in November 1994, my young sister, Abigail Ntombu Yikona, (Mrs. Chintu) our seventh born, died in London. Abigail was also a graduate from the University of Zambia. Again, I had to ask for compassionate leave as well as permission from Nottingham Trent University to accompany my late sister's body to Zambia. I had not taken preventative measures against malaria. November is a period of heavy rain in Zambia, especially Mwinilunga. I accompanied

my sister Abigail to her preferred place of rest in Mwinilunga, Zambia. This wish was clearly stated in her lasting will. All families and friends were supportive at the funeral and united in strong prayer for peace and blessings for those left behind. At Abigail's request, Nelson and I were to raise her son Mambwe. Mambwe is now a fine young gentleman and working in the UK.

When Mambwe was nine months old I cut his hair, this was the first time it had been cut, his parents waited for an elder to carry this out. I introduced him to solids and in the traditional way, I fed him Nshima (maize meal and water).

I looked after Mambwe when his mother was ill. When he became our son he was three years old. He did very well at school and was always close to his father Nelson. He studied sport psychology and now works at the Nottingham University in the sports department.

Following my return to the UK in December 1994, I became very ill with malaria. Initially, the clinical team were reluctant to accept this diagnosis despite my exposure to mosquitoes in Zambia. The blood test results confirmed malaria. Meanwhile my young brother, Dr. Joseph Yikona came from Sheffield and encouraged the doctors to treat me vigorously with anti-malarial drugs and intravenous fluids. My brother had worked in Zambia and fully understood the management of some tropical diseases and their complications.

Sometimes professionals believe in themselves to the extent that they are slow to listen and actually hear what the patient is saying. There is then delay in treatment, which can be fatal. Being a registered nurse and teacher, and having taught about malaria in great detail, I knew some of the causes, signs and symptoms well. Whilst in D57, the ward where I was admitted, I imparted this knowledge to some registrars, junior doctors and the nurses before I was discharged. The staff were overwhelmed and grateful. Malaria is an infectious disease prevalent in Mwinilunga, the area that I had just visited.

Whilst an in-patient my friends and relatives visited and this made me feel much better. Physically I was shivering, my husband Nelson innocently brought extra blankets to cover me, but the nurse wisely told him not to do so. I had a high temperature and the body shivers to get rid of the heat. Nelson is very caring but possibly not a budding nurse.

Following my return to work the lecturers at Trent University and the managers at Queen's Medical Centre were all supportive and allowed me to continue with work as well as my studies.

Additional Developments and Courses

From 21st April 1995 there was a three day IONA Conference held in Nottingham which included a special civic reception and cocktail party at the Nottingham City Council House, in the presence of the Lord Mayor and City Councilors.

As an IONA life member I look forward to their annual conferences held in different locations within the UK and abroad. One year, with the help of Nelson, I compiled a crossword for the IONA Newsletter.

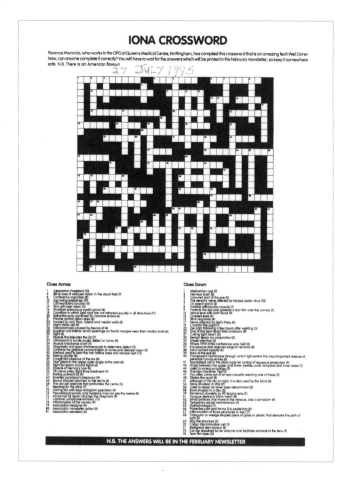

Loss of my brother Richard

At the end of February 1996 I lost my immediate elder brother Richard Michael Dikimbi Kazembi Yikona, the fourth born. He graduated from the University of Zambia in Economics and Public Administration. He then went on to study the Post Railway Marketing Educational Programme in Canada. In earlier days, my brother and Nelson had played football together and they were in the Zambian national team.

I was helped at this time by my friend Maureen Smith.

"We have flown free from their fangs, free of their traps, free as a bird. Their grip is broken. We are free as a bird in flight" Psalm 124:7

In 1996 while working in ophthalmic outpatients, I gathered information and to help them approach and communicate with the visually impaired.

With the support of Angela Waters, (originally from Jamaica) a colleague who had been in the department longer than me, we produced a basic orientation and information pack for student nurses and new staff. I also included a terminology booklet for new staff and the clinic receptionists.

I continued to actively seek educative opportunities for myself. I attended a comprehensive study day on intravenous technique and the use of pump and controllers. This study involved taking an exam at the end, which I passed.

I completed the Diploma in Higher Education Health Studies in December 1996. The following year I commenced a Degree in Health Care at Derby University and completed it in 1998.

As part of my role I completed a learning package. It contained information on cannulation and the administration of diagnostic fluorescein for ophthalmic angiograms performing minor operations such as chalazion and skin tag removal. I drew up allocation timetables for students coming to the eye clinic on placement, as well as providing ad-hoc teaching sessions in the School of Nursing when required.

I started updating orientation packages for new staff, students and nursing auxiliaries. The head of Professional Development and Co-ordinator Pauline Tweedale, supported the documentation and encouraged it to be used in clinical areas to ensure students got the most out of the learning opportunities available in ophthalmology. Not only did The Nottingham Faculty of Medicines and Health Sciences and The School of Nursing and Midwifery benefit, but also visitors to the clinic area.

In April 1996 together with other staff from eye casualty and eye clinic, I went to the Radcliffe Infirmary, Oxford to take part in a study. The topics included corneal and diabetic nursing roles; developing nurse-led clinics and the use of visual aids.

In July, I attended a Blood Glucose Monitoring Training session on the Reflolux system at Queen's Medical Centre. In October, I attended an assessor's workshop on the Project 2000 course. The programme included assessment of clinical practice and specific branches such as Adult, Child, Mental Health and Learning Disabilities.

I was spending some of my clinical sessions with the anesthetists in ophthalmic theatres to be taught and in my own time during breaks, I observed the nurse practitioner in Adult Accident and Emergency at QMC. I also practiced with junior doctors, registrars and consultants in eye clinic.

In February 1997 I visited South Africa with Dr. Paula Gormley. On 10th February, I was asked to give a fifteen minute talk to nurses at the Medical School, University of Pretoria, on Community Eye Health. I recalled my practice whilst in Zambia, where I had been involved in sporadic mobile clinics. I also gave an example of some of the clinical officers and ophthalmic nurses trained in Malawi who were able to do refractions as well as cataract operations. The talk was followed by a lengthy discussion so my spot lasted for a combined total of 45 minutes but everyone was pleased with what had been discussed.

Miss Gormley and I participated in a 'cataract camp' based in the Northern Province at Nylstroom District Hospital, where we screened, selected and confirmed diagnoses. Out of this insightful visit, I was able to present a paper and poster in the year 2000, at the IONA Conference which ran for two days. The members appreciated my presentation and the poster was distributed on request. Miss Gormley then went on Safari in South Africa and I returned home to carry on with my degree.

On 11th April 1997 I attended The IONA conference held held at Riccarton Campus, Herriot Watt University, Edinburgh, Scotland, along with colleagues Sue Ashby and Margaret Harman. The conference was attended by delegates from Nigeria, the United States of America (USA) and Eire (Republic of Ireland) amongst others. The topics of discussion included the launch of the Ophthalmic Nursing Journal, The Nurses' Role in Ophthalmic Outpatients, The Effects of Sleep Deprivation, Patients Undergoing Intensive Eye Drop Therapy, A Nurse-led Support Service for Oncology Patients and Developing the Nurse Practitioner Role.

Warrington Wet Laboratory (Wet Lab)

On 4th July 1998 I was sponsored by Mr. Galloway, a consultant at the QMC, to attend a study day at Warrington Hospital Ophthalmic Centre. I and other nurses spent the day in wet lab where we learnt about the making of a small incision done in cataract surgery. Wet lab represented a wonderful opportunity for nurses' skills development and professional prospect including through the practice of a routine operation normally performed by an ophthalmic surgeon.

A cataract extraction and insertion of intraocular lens implant was demonstrated. This helped the ophthalmic theatre nurse to understand the procedure and the instruments used. It also assisted the nurse in explaining the procedure to the patients going on the waiting list, thus helping to allay any anxiety.

1999 was a year of significant professional advances as well as challenges that affected nurses.

I became a Clinical Nurse Practitioner.

BSc (Hons) Healthcare/Grandmother

I graduated from Derby University in January 1999 with a degree in Health Care. That same month, my first grandson was born. Dryden Anthony Mwando was born on the 4th January 1999 we were very proud to name him after both my father and his mother's father. As a first-time grandmother, I delighted in my new role. The latter combined with my extensive clinical and educational experiences, contributed to make my life ever challenging and interesting.

At a professional level, this was a time when I learnt in detail how to provide clinical support and gained further skills in the supervision of students in both general adult nursing and ophthalmology. I was also fully active in connecting with other units in ophthalmology both in the UK and abroad.

Sailas

The father of my first grandson is Sailas. He is our first born son. I was forced to leave Sailas with my mother and father for a time to concentrate on starting and developing my career. I did this for the sake of the whole family, to give all my children a better upbringing. I missed him, however, this was tempered somewhat by the fact that I knew he was getting the best attention full-time from my parents and part-time the occasions when his father visited him.

He is now the father of two sons Dryden Anthony Mwando and Lovell Nelson Mwando, who are growing into fine young men.

I love him for his kindness and generosity, these are traits that I am sure came from my parents. I am very proud of him.

Becoming a grandmother and obtaining my degree were very special occasions and good reasons for celebration. Celebrations are an effective way for family members to bond while enjoying the company of friends and colleagues. By celebrating together, we create precious memories which will later bring great joy. Praise be to God for giving us such blessings and for keeping this united family in harmony.

The knowledge and skills I obtained through my university education became very useful in preparing my personal lesson sheet to carry our fluorescein angiography. Despite having gone through fairly recent bereavement, I managed to concentrate on my clinical practice and education, something some of my friends and colleagues at work would admire.

Some of the literature review I came across highlights that "many professionals do not know what to say when comforting the bereaved" (Becker and Gamlin 2004). I had never realised that until I lost a number of family members including brothers, sisters, father, mother, in laws.

Looking back now, I think I didn't need to be so concerned about what I or others said or didn't in those moments as silence can be a positive thing. Becker and Gamblin(2004) commented that people can do a lot of useful thinking in silent moments, and sometimes we should resist the urge to speak.

Cardiff Congress

On 19th-21st of May 1999, the Royal College of Ophthalmologists Annual Congress was held in Cardiff. This was the first time that nurses were allocated a day for study and participation. On the 19th of May we commenced the morning session with a symposium which involved ophthalmologists, optometrists, orthoptists and nurses.

Colleagues Keith knox, Elizabeth Naylor and I had an opportunity to attend. We discussed with nurses from other units on how nurse-led clinics were established and approved by their medical colleagues.

International Health Exchange

In August 2000 the International Health Exchange organised courses such as Health Care in Emergencies, Culture, Communication and Health Risk Management. These courses were relevant to anyone intending to work abroad as well as in the UK - especially in the voluntary sector.

From 20th - 22nd October 2000 (as a member of the International Health Exchange) I attended a Health and Safety Course in Birmingham. The course covered health and safety, drug management and dealing with displaced people, such as those in war and natural disasters (floods or wide spread disease).

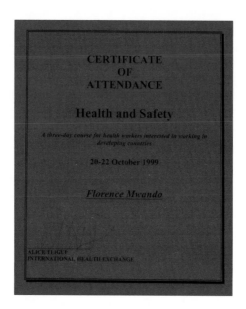

CERTIFICATE
OF
ATTENDANCE

Health and Safety

A three-day course for health workers interested in working in developing countries

20-22 October 1999

Florence Mwando

ALICE ELLGUE
INTERNATIONAL HEALTH EXCHANGE

Clinical Nurse Practitioner

I spent the rest of the year concentrating on my role as Clinical Nurse Practitioner.

On the 12th October I attended World Sight Day in London, and to mark the occasion, the ophthalmology section of The Royal Society of Medicine held a meeting at the Royal Society in London. Colleagues Keith Knox, Carol Bullock and I attended the multi-disciplinary meeting where the majority of those present were ophthalmologists. Speakers emphasised that the prevention of blindness worldwide was a critical issue and that it would be better tackled now than in 2020. Health care professionals and myself, as an ophthalmic nurse, were aware of the consequences of systemic diseases. Conditions such as diabetes and the effects of ageing are some of the contributing problems to blindness and could be prevented or solved.

Other speakers spoke on the need to promote linkage programmes and training requirements - which should include research methodology and evaluation of outcomes including prospective monitoring of cataract, major childhood blinding diseases and their prevention worldwide, the importance of developing human and other material resources and the importance of research funding.

In October 2000, I joined the Institute for Learning and Teaching (ILT). ILT was one of the organisations responsible for supporting excellence in learning and teaching in the UK. I attended their short courses and meetings to enhance my educational development and assessment skills. In my opinion, the membership fees were good value for money. In 2007 I was recognised as Fellow of the Higher Education Academy. It took seven years to finally achieve this status.

Macular Service

During the year 2000 an extensive ophthalmic research on Age-Related Macular Degeneration (AMD) and how to manage it took place. ADM involved the intervention by a medical ophthalmic doctor to do photodynamic therapy and intravitreal injections (PDT/IVI). In November, my colleague Keith Knox and I went to Shropshire for a study day on age-related macular disease sponsored by Novartis Ophthalmics. The course included the use of LogMar charts for testing vision and preparation of visudyne. A photodynamic therapy was extremely beneficial, and a mode of backup for ophthalmic managers to support the establishment of a macular clinic.

By 2001 some patients were selected through special criteria to be treated by one of these methods and only a few nurses assisted their medical colleagues. I was one of the interested nurses to participate.

Due to recent developments, the patients were able to be carefully selected and screened.

Patients were seen on Monday evening clinics and treated on Saturdays following the results of their fluorescein angiogram results.

In May 2001 colleagues Keith Knox, Frances Osborn and I attended the Annual Ophthalmological Congress in Birmingham. This resulted in great things in ophthalmology! Due to innovations and research needs, new consultants and fellows were recruited.

In July, I was nominated to the International Ophthalmic Nurses Council and was given the role of Publicity Officer. I was confirmed into the council during the York I.O.N.A. Conference. I recruited many colleagues, both in Nottingham and outside, to become members.

As a Clinical Nurse Practitioner in eye outpatients at the Queen's Medical Centre, I had opportunities to meet pharmaceutical colleagues who sponsored and provided various visual aids and current ophthalmic preparations to meet the growing demand of eye patients with acute or long term visual problems such as diabetes, glaucoma, cataracts, cornea and iris inflammation as well as eyelid and conjunctival complications. This also gave me chances to invite them to I.O.N.A. conferences.

2 INTOUCH ■ SEPTEMBER • 2001 – ISSUE 12

Florence is appointed to IONA

Florence Mwando, clinical nurse practitioner in eye outpatients here at Queen's, has been appointed to the Council of the International Ophthalmic Nurses' Association (IONA).

Florence has worked at Queen's for nine years and is delighted to have been appointed onto the IONA council - the association which was founded in 1955 to provide an opportunity for ophthalmic nurses world wide to share knowledge and experience.

IONA provides an independent voice to promote the value of the ophthalmic nurse.

NUH Article September 2001

The workload increased in outpatients as did the number of consultants and their specialist clinics. The relationship between the medical colleagues, optometrists, orthoptics and nurses grew stronger. Fluorescein angiograms were increasingly carried out on more and more patients. The advantage of the procedure was rapid results, which in turn enabled medical colleagues to make quick diagnoses and manage their clinics smoothly. Some minor eyelid conditions were referred to my list for surgery. I carried this out in clinic on Wednesday afternoons and Friday mornings with the support of the specialist registrars and some consultants. I was advised when to operate or refer if the problem needed to be dealt with in main theatres. I also taught colleagues and students in the School of Nursing.

By June 2001, an ophthalmic consultant manifested a special interest to work with a team in running a clinic for all patients suitable for photodynamic therapy. The team was also fully dedicated to the macular service, receiving referrals from other hospitals. Nottingham was one of the main ophthalmology centres.

In November, The Elizabeth Thomas Seminar on Macular Degeneration Diseases was held in Nottingham. I had obtained sufficient sponsorship funding for myself and some other colleagues from the QMC to attend. Originally, I was supposed to go to a conference in Boston USA, however, this was at the time of 9/11 and I was unable to fly.

In 2002, after renewing my three-year periodic United Kingdom Central Council for Nursing, Midwifery and Health Visiting (UKCC) membership, I continued to support students and extend my clinical skills to other ophthalmic areas, such as the wards. I carefully assessed the competencies and supervision skills of mentors and followed student nurses undertake their ophthalmic placements, ensuring outcomes were achieved and signed off by their mentor.

My confidence in carrying out minor operations and diagnostic fluorescein angiography were becoming stronger and more efficient, so much so that patients remarked *"you can do this with your eyes shut"*. However, I did not attempt it!

Update on Community Eye Health Matters

In April the staff and Management Committee of the International Health Exchange invited me to their 21st Annual General Meeting (in the presence of HRH The Princess Royal) to the Royal College of Nursing in London. The meeting was about the various challenges of communicable diseases and control in complex emergencies. The speakers represented the World Health Organisation (WHO) and Health Net International. This was and is up to this day, one of the most memorable evenings of my life.

This is a treasured photograph of me at the Royal College of Nursing (RCN) with President, Roswyn Hakesley-Brown. I am wearing a traditional African dress.

During the questions and answers session, the audience and panel were given an opportunity to participate in a debate on the themes of the meeting. I presented a question regarding the awareness of Chlamydia and sexual health. One of my interests was the nature of trachoma which leads to blindness and complications. Chlamydia is a well-known communicable disease but its link as one of the major causes of trachoma may be overlooked. I was fortunate that Professor Harminda S Dua was able to help me understand the subject well, as he is an expert in this field.

Although my role as a nurse involved numerous duties, I strived to ensure that I had a balanced workload at the local, national and international levels whilst maintaining professional high standards and providing my patients with the highest level of care. I cannot recall ever having any complaints come my way, so hopefully I achieved this.

At the same time, as a housewife and mother, when not working, I cooked special meals both for my husband and children, and visiting relatives and friends. My husband and I have always eaten at home as it is cheaper than going out or ordering take-aways. Furthermore, I have allergies to some foods - especially to some plastic tasting type-foods!

I was aware that in order to perform my duties to the best of my abilities I had to achieve a balanced home/work life. However, this did not stop me from bringing work home sometimes. In the evenings before bedtime but after the children were settled, I undertook such tasks as preparing my student/mentor allocations and the concomitant work associated with it. Preparations take a long time but are worthwhile in clinical settings. Students, colleagues and myself would all be able to use and build on the benefits.

In December 2002 Keith Knox, Ian Smith and I published a Research Audit of nurse-led diagnosis of chalazia in Ophthalmic Nursing Journal Vol. 6 Issue 3.

RCN Membership and Work

In 2003 I joined the Royal College of Nursing. Prior to this I was in UNISON. I was practicing in a substantive post where I took on more responsibility. This required the use of extensive educational materials so having use of their library was a real bonus.

On 31st of August my mother, Fonisiya Yihemba Yikona, passed away after attending a church conference in Mwinilunga. Mum had a strong will and was a very able person. She cared for my father and her ten children, and even though she never had a paid job, people came to our house so that she could deliver their babies. In later life she helped to translate the English bible into lunda – our local language.

"This is my covenant with them" says the lord. *"My spirit will not leave them, and neither will these words I have given you. They will be on your lips and on the lips of your children and your children's children forever."* Isaiah 59:21

I still remember my mother's words of wisdom, given freely to me throughout my life.

I had a comprehensive Individual Performance Management appraisal in December, which was to be reviewed in January 2005. One of my stated goals was to strengthen the educational role for all staff and students, including professional visitors. The envisaged result of this was to build on the excellent status of the ophthalmic unit at the Queen's Medical Centre.

Another career direction discussed was the possibility of my writing a book which would include my experiences of being a nurse. I knew that if I undertook this challenge it would be time consuming and very personal, but I thought it would only be a matter of time before I embarked on such a mission. On November 11th I successfully received my updated Resuscitation Training in Adult Hospital Life Support. This is one of the many mandatory ongoing courses needed to be completed by all staff working as nurse practitioners.

On Saturday November 29th some of my colleagues and I went to Manchester Royal Eye Hospital to attend the National Ophthalmic Nurses study day and exhibition. The eye clinic is closed at weekends so this gave us an opportunity to have an enjoyable team-building day out together whilst at the same time updating our knowledge.

The study day focused on extending specific roles and specialism to meet public demand. One aspect covered was 'Cataract Management - present and future', and there were workshop sessions on Biometry, Focimetry and Keratometry. Attending the study day helped build creativity, innovation and motivation into our ophthalmic work, such as the establishment of the nurse-led clinics.

In the same period I compiled a booklet of terminology, and ordered and paid for copies to be delivered to myself on behalf of the ophthalmic unit. I thought that this would be useful and beneficial for unqualified medical people who would have something to refer to if needed. Also, the Nottingham School of Nursing and clinical practice areas established links and named contacts for supporting and mentoring student nurses.

The 2003 Staff Award Scheme celebrating individual and team contributions Certificate of Recognition, signed by both the Chairman and Chief Executive of the QMC, was awarded to the Ophthalmic, ENT and Neuro Practice Learning team in grateful recognition of their valued contribution to patient care. It was great for our work and effort to be recognised.

As an IONA Life Member I attended an interesting conference and annual dinner in Edinburgh.

In 2004 I progressed to Practice Development Nurse (Pre-Registration Lead). The role was 40% hands-on clinical care at a specialist level, the remaining 60% being allocated to:

a) Designing, delivering and evaluating teaching programmes for pre-registration students allocated to all clinical areas within the ophthalmology directorate;

b) Organising mentors and assessors for clinical supervision;

c) Updating unit staff on all aspects of the Diploma of Nursing Programme and their responsibilities to student learning;

d) Administrative duties such as monitoring all records, creating and maintaining a database of study day, mentors, updates and links to the School of Nursing.

I contributed to the organisation of the first Nottingham Ophthalmic Nursing Study Day (on my birthday) held in the Eye and ENT Seminar room on the 6th of July. This was a day of which I am immensely proud.

I made up a practical role play together with Cathryn Willbond for the macular clinic. It included performing the LogMar vision test and a fluorescein angiogram. On top of being a fun thing to do, it was also an effective learning tool and had a strong impact. It not only delivered practical knowledge of a procedure but also an overall awareness of the workings of the macular clinic. I even incorporated language difficulties to overcome.

On 26th August I attended an infusion device teaching session, held in the Medical Equipment Supply Unit Department. I received essential training on the use of Graseby 500 Volumetric Pump and Graseby 3100 Syringe Pump. This was part of an update to ensure safety in carrying out fluorescein angiograms and photodynamic therapy. Sometimes I feel I can describe myself as understanding technology!

In the same year I worked on secondment with the East Midlands Royal College of Nursing. I was the lead on the equality and diversity programme as a Regional Advisor. Awareness of diversity improves care. I organised the content and delivery of the courses. The training was initially for staff in Ophthalmology, Ear, Nose & Throat as well as theatres. It was so successful that it was expanded to include the rest of the hospital. Even the clinical director asked to attend. It was then taken to the other nine regional branches of the East Midlands. Following on from this, people from other areas of Britain expressed in interest in the programme. Its aim was to help staff to understand different cultures, religions and health delivery for people with a disability - mainly for the visually impaired and hard of hearing. The training included definitions and input on equality and diversity, European equal treatment, legislation on disability, human rights, race relations and sex discrimination.

I also helped support the immigrant nurses in their endeavours to adapt. Having been in their position myself, I was able to understand the difficulties of settling down in the UK when from abroad and empathise. Keith Burrell, one of the Anti-Racist and Diversity Training Officers from Manchester was invited to come to Nottingham East Midlands Regional Office to talk to RCN staff from Nottingham, Birmingham and Derby. Keith was an independent social expert who had interesting and pertinent facts and issues to present.

Keith's training objectives were to enable the participants to:

- Value diversity at work within the RCN
- Understand self and others within a diverse workforce
- Appreciate and value differences
- Examine useful strategies for practice development
- Discuss the associated various Acts of law
  - ➤ Sex Discrimination Act 1975 and 1976
  - ➤ Race Relations Act 1976 Amended 2000
  - ➤ Equal Pay Act 1980 Amended 1983
  - ➤ Disability Act 1944 Amended 1995
  - ➤ Human Rights Act 1998
  - ➤ Criminal Justice Act 1998
- Outline the Commission for Racial Equality document.

I organised the fourth diversity network entitled 'Pushing Ahead', held at the White Hart, Nottingham on the 29th July. We had common themes, which were looking into the needs of internationally recruited nurses and refugee nurses. We also examined and exchanged the experiences of nurses' unique skill competencies which could be shared to improve patient outcomes. Two of the topics discussed were ethics and etiquette.

It was amazing that Jennifer Doohan – the RCN Professional Development Officer and I had actually attended the International Council for Nurses (ICN) in Geneva and obtained a copy of the Code of Ethics for Nurses. We were able to refer to this and share our experiences with my colleagues and the student nurses. An international code of ethics for nurses was first adopted by the ICN in 1953. It states that "Nurses have four fundamental responsibilities; to promote health, to prevent illness, to restore health and to alleviate suffering. The need for nursing is universal".

Two colleagues and I attended the 'Access to Health in Developing Countries' Conference held at the Royal College of Nursing (RCN) in London, and chaired by RCN President Sylvia Denton. The conference was held under the auspices of the International Council of Nurses, the International Confederation, and the International Network of the Availability of Scientific Publications, and was sponsored by the British Medical Journal.

It was discussed and agreed that local nurses and midwives must be consulted about information required and in what format, and it was decided that the provision of information should be suitable in local languages, as well as in other languages other than English.

During the International Nurses Day in May the following year, the theme focused on "Nurses Working Against Poverty". The ICN quoted Mahatma Ghandi who stated that "Poverty is the worst form of violence" and the greatest misery we face today. As nurses we know that investing in education, healthcare and sound social policy is of paramount importance because they can improve health outcomes. We also know that health is an asset, but they all overlap.

By 2005 I was proficient at supporting junior doctors in their practice of carrying out minor eyelid operations, as part of my role I confirmed their safe performance to the appropriate teams for approved competencies.

On the 3rd of May I attended the 'Two Centuries of Vision' (Bi-centenary 1805 – 2005) at Moorfields Eye Hospital in London. This was an exceptional opportunity to meet ophthalmic professionals, and some of IONA members from the USA.

In October 2004 former Kitwe and Mufulira Zambian nurses met in London to honour Mr. Zzizinga at a surprise event for all that he had done. The main organisers were Caroline Muchelemba, Sally, Monde, Pricilla Mayanda, Christine Sakulanda and and myself amongst others.

Another Death and Passport Confusion

On Friday the 15th of May, whilst working in the eye clinic, I received a phone call to say that my elder sister, the second born in our family, had died in a 'mine' hospital in Kitwe. These hospitals were open to mine workers and their relatives. Evah Kaluswika Yikona (Mrs. Kanombe) was a graduate of the University of Zambia and Leeds University, UK. She was the headmistress at Mindolo Girls School in Kitwe where I attended prior to entering into nursing in 1972. Evah was more than a biological elder sister to me; she was like my second mother and I was more than devastated, so much so that words aren't enough to describe.

I felt helpless and could not come to terms with why this was happening. I asked God: "where are you?" I was so distressed by the news of her death that I took the wrong passport to the travel agent to buy a ticket to go to Zambia. As a responsible mother I kept everyone's documents. On this day, my daughter Lydia's passport was in a black case like mine. My husband and I were in the travel agents and bought the air ticket and handed over what I

thought was my passport when it was in fact my daughter's passport. The sales' agent returned the passport and printed the ticket. My husband, Nelson and I came back home where friends and relatives from London and Nottingham had gathered. Suddenly, Nelson who was checking the tickets exclaimed "Bana, Sailas, this is written Lydia!" I was shocked! Nelson immediately returned to the travel agent to explain to the sales' assistant what was wrong with the issued ticket when I was meant to travel less than 24 hours later! Despite our best effort to convince the travel agent we had made a silly mistake due to the shock caused

by the news of the death of a relative, the travel agent refused to change the ticket. This was hard... and with commercial regulations, even in time of death, we were told to buy another ticket. The following day we went to London and bought another ticket with the help of friends Mr. and Mrs. Phiri, who negotiated with a sales' travel agent they knew. My training as a nurse and ability to deal with emergency situations did not help me here!

I travelled safely to Zambia and on my return, went back to work. I brought back the funeral programme and the wrong ticket to show to the travel agent and also contacted the International Air Transport Association, who successfully advised me accordingly and after almost six months, I received a refund and sympathy letter from the airline. Eventually, with the support of family and friends and my faith I got through this sad time in my life.

Organisation of Local Ophthalmic Study Days 2006

In July some colleagues and I organised the second ophthalmic study day which was held in the Post Graduate Education Centre, QMC.

My main role in this was dealing with the financial aspects such as raising enough money to run the course. To this end, I applied for funding and support from the pharmaceutical exhibitors. I was determined the event would be successful. I also contributed a power point presentation and made up a role play on 'Appreciating Diversity and Racial Awareness'. Our ophthalmic staff presentations were well liked as demonstrated by the evaluations submitted by the delegates. This was perhaps due to the injection of humour. We were advised to put it on at The Theatre Royal.

On the 22nd of July I received an acknowledgement letter from the Head Nurse/Matron Ann Watts which said, *"Thank you, the role play at the beginning was certainly a talking point amongst the audience, together with the serious message imparted by the slides."*

At this time, following the discussions at the Ophthalmic, ENT and Neuro Practice Learning Team meetings from 2005, we worked on how best to achieve the issues discussed. These were the developments and commitments around placements and how best students can be supported to achieve the relevant outcomes.

From this, we established sessions whereby students from different specialisms presented practical demonstrations of what they had learnt during their placement. For example, ENT students presented the care of tracheostomies, epistaxis and oral hygiene. Shared sessions incorporated some common factors such as the healing process and the promotion of health education.

These best-sharing methods of assessment, evaluation and achievement of their outcomes, was one of the best ways of learning.

I attended a mandatory Conflict Resolution Training Session, which had to be undertaken every three years.

At the same time, I supported colleagues from other ophthalmic units such as the Pilgrim hospital in Lincolnshire, the Kings Lynn hospital in Norfolk and others Leicestershire and Derbyshire. This was usually by teaching procedures and guidelines. It covered issues such as consenting, health and safety issues (especially on sharps policy and waste management), incident reporting, cannulation and incision and curettage of minor cases.

On the 8th of June I completed a one day course on the Role of the Coroner and Giving Evidence, which was certified by H.M. Coroner for Nottinghamshire. All of the previously documented courses and study days show the breadth and depth of knowledge a senior nurse has to have in order to effectively carry out her role.

On the 13th of October I had the pleasure of attending another Elizabeth Thomas Seminar at the East Midlands Conference Centre in Nottingham. This increased my knowledge on macular conditions and their management because I learnt the latest updates on the causes and different types of macular degeneration and new treatments available. These annual seminars are expensive, but provide a wealth of knowledge and maintain the credibility to practice in ophthalmic nursing.

Also in 2006, student support in their practice placements was highly needed, but there was an overall dearth of mentors. This was dealt with by the introduction of the Befriender Scheme. The scheme allowed level two and three nursing auxiliaries to act as a friend to the student, and work with them. The teaching of practical and technical skills and the facilitation of the students' learning remained the responsibility of the students' mentor. This scheme had limitations due to the restrictions surrounding what the student could actually learn from the auxiliary. My role was to prepare all of the auxiliaries.

My Son's Graduation

I attended the Graduation of my son, Samonu Mwando, at the Headingley Campus of Leeds Metropolitan University on the 24th November. He graduated with a BSc (Hons) in Computing. Nelson and I as well as the rest of my family are proud of Samonu's achievement. His qualification assisted him to gain his independence from home, and today Samonu lives in Leeds working as a Recruitment Consultant. Below is a picture of us at Samonu's graduation with my sister-in-law Diniwe Yikona.

The Nursing and Midwifery Council (2006) brought out a booklet entitled 'Standards to Support Learning and Assessment in Practice: NMC Standards for Mentors, Practice Teachers and Teachers'. In response to this a Mentorship Bulletin was issued by the Nottingham University School of Nursing, starting in January 2007. I was responsible for the database of mentors and linked up with the School of Nursing.

Another change in documentation at this time was the introduction of 'The Scope of Working in New Ways' packages for staff nurses. The filled-in documents ensured that venepuncture and cannulation training was completed on time to commence fluorescein angiograms. I was responsible for record keeping.

I also organised the training of all staff in the conversion of our Snellen visual-type testing to LogMar testing and the recording of near visions of a reading chart. I would like to acknowledge Professor Martin Rubinstein who actually taught me. We then assessed each staff member together.

On the 26th of January I attended the 11th Nottingham Eye Symposium and Research Meeting. This meeting was extremely interesting as up-to-date current research was presented. Eye specialists from all over the world attended.

The meeting I went to in March entitled 'Advances in Corneal Therapy' showcased at the East Midlands Conference Centre. New treatments and their effectiveness were discussed in detail. These conferences are stimulating and can give one renewed energy to perform at their best.

Also In March I was thrilled to achieve the status of Fellow of the Higher Education Academy. This made me feel very proud!

An AMD Nurse Symposium was held in Birmingham on 30th June, and I attended with several colleagues. This enhanced our progress in Nottingham in developing photodynamic therapy for patients, as this symposium was extremely detailed.

2007 – NHSP Nursing Agency and
Voluntary Support for Colleagues in Zambia

In October 2007, although I remained full-time in the ophthalmology department, I joined the National Health Service Professionals (NHSP) nursing agency in order to generate additional income for my family. This would help me support my children in their studies and pay for the shipping of educational materials I had been collecting to Zambia.

Whilst working with the Royal College of Nursing in Nottingham, East Midlands Regional Office, I organised and collected numerous donated magazines and nursing journals, and medical and nursing books – with the assistance of several colleagues.

When I visited staff and students in different schools of nursing in Zambia (especially in Kitwe and the University Teaching Hospital in Lusaka, which I had visited after the death of my elder sister), I found the library shelves empty of reading and educational materials. I decided to help! I worked forty-five shifts in the Adult Accident and Emergency Department and earned enough to pay air freight for the materials to Zambia. My sister (cousin), Dr. Beatrice Chifwelu (Mrs. Amadi) agreed to keep them in her house and by July she had distributed them to the UTH. As an educator, I knew the benefits of education.

'We make a living by what we get, but we make a life by what we give'.
(Winston Churchill).

What I did was published in 'NUHorizons', a Nottingham University Hospitals publication. In response to this I kindly received an email from some members of staff from the QMC.

"Hi, Florence. Guess what – just been looking at this week's Trust Briefing and you are the heroine of the week! Well done Florence, it was great to read all about your fantastic achievements and your kindness and effort that you made for Zambia. We are so proud of you! And all those extra hours you worked on Zambia's behalf, you are a truly good person and I feel privileged to know you Florence. Just felt I had to write and tell you what a wonderful lady you are. All the Best, Nina x."

I am very grateful for positive feedback and words of affirmation I receive. I strive to provide a thorough and caring service because I love what I do and do it wholeheartedly! Positive words of encouragement in return has helped me in my practice and contributed to raising my confidence and self-esteem. Making a positive difference in people's life remains nevertheless my highest motivational factor.

On 8th May 2008, the department previously referred to as eyes, ENT and maxillofacial, now renamed 'Head and Neck' set up a meeting to discuss the 'Essential Skills Clusters' required for assessment entry to the branch programme (such as the adult branch).

A year later, in May 2009, I attended an Advanced Life Support course together with other nurses, pharmacists and doctors. We were taught how to use a defibrillator and how to deal with severe anaphylaxis. This built upon my autonomous nurse practitioner role while carrying out minor operations and fluorescein angiograms. This course was consented for self-evaluation through the media of video, which would also be used on future courses.

I completed a Cytotoxic Drug Collection and Handling assessment. This allowed me to be proficient in the collection and use of cytotoxic drugs. Sometimes they were prescribed for use in clinic or ophthalmic theatre for the treatment or preventative management of conditions such as glaucoma.

Head and Neck Study Day

Along with some others, on November 26th, I organised the first 'Nottingham Head and Neck Emergencies in the 21st Century' Conference. It was held at the Post Graduate Multidisciplinary Education Centre, QMC Campus. Delegates came from all over the country. They represented Ophthalmology, ENT, Maxillofacial and Adult Accident and Emergency Departments. Most of the speakers came from the QMC, but we had an interesting talk from the Coroner of Nottingham, Dr. Nigel Chapman. We also had a very moving talk from Mr. Tom McInulty, a representative from the Macular Disease Society, who was accompanied by his guide dog. His   presentation was on his personal experiences and proved effective in raising awareness on individual treatment needs.

This conference was very well supported and sponsored by eleven pharmaceutical exhibitors. The final evaluations were excellent and the delegates requested to have another conference.

As a result of this Study Day, those that attended, including myself, were awarded six category points. These points are essential for revalidation as well as renewal of registration for the fitness to practice

Lydia and Evahs' Graduation

My vision, on professional and personal grounds, is firmly rooted in the importance of education. This extends to all the children in my family who I actively encourage to study. Unconsciously, I believe this might have impacted on both my girls who successfully achieved academically. I have experience of both the Zambian and UK education systems, which I both admire for various reasons. I was immensely proud when both girls obtained degrees. I am still proud of them!

Both my daughters graduated on the same day, the 15th of July 2009. Evah Kaluswika Mwando graduated from All Saints, Leeds University having obtained a BSc (Hons) Psychology and Media. Lydia Kaji Mantabe Mwando went to the DeMontfort University, Leicester and studied engineering and information technology. My daughters asked to have their graduations on different days, but of course it was not possible! As a united family we split up to attend both girls' award ceremony. The women in the family went to

Leicester whilst the men went to Leeds. I do not know what the rest of the graduates of Leeds University thought of Evah surrounded by all those men! By 5pm, we all gathered in front of the Queen's Medical Centre to have family photographs taken with the girls.

Nelson also values education. He is a loving father to our children and cares a great deal about all family members. He spent time teaching our children mathematics, and ensured order and respect was paramount. Nelson made it clear to the children that "every champion needs a coach and if you do not work hard and get a job you will not eat". We ensured there was financial backing from us but it came with responsibilities – the children had to be focused and make us proud. I feel as a family we are achieving a lot because like my mother and father, we are hard-working and aim to succeed. I can also see that this is still happening with the younger generation.

We had a family party to celebrate Mambwe's birthday together with all the graduates whose achievement we wanted to celebrate. This said, while proud of the academic achievements of family members who have chosen that route, I am also proud of those who have opted for a different path than the academic route and chosen not to go to university. A good work ethic is not only reflected in academia but in character and personality, and regardless of our chosen field and levels of education, our inner worth is more than grades and test results! And so, I wish to also applaud those family members without a university education who have become professionals in their own rights, making a positive contribution to society or in the process of getting there!

Educational Trip to Zambia

Furthermore, in May, I gave a presentation about Zambian Nurse Education. It was sponsored by the RCN East Midlands Regional Office to mark International Nurses Day. This also helped me to prepare for an educational trip to Zambia that I planned to take. Attendees were requested to donate any books and journals that could be taken to Zambia, and cakes were being sold to raise funds for shipping. I was very grateful to the RCN for organising the event which benefited both the staff and students in Zambia.

In August 2010, I retired. We then concentrated on getting these materials to the places where they would have an impact. In September, Nelson went to Zambia and collected the educational materials and took them to Dr. Amadi's house for storage. It cost a lot of money in taxes and freight charges!

In October, I travelled to Zambia with four colleagues, Peggy Katambi, Julian Luwaya, Loveness Shaba and Ann Watts. We distributed the books and journals to the UTH, Chainama Hills Psychiatric Hospital and the Ndola, Mufulira and Kitwe Schools of Nursing on the Copper Belt.

Another Family Death

On my return from Zambia and only when reaching Heathrow Airport, I received a text from my nephew George Noel Kanombe informing me that Peggy, my niece, (his wife) who had been driving us around in Zambia, had passed away after being bitten by a poisonous snake. This was a shock and very distressing. She was a beautiful soul. "Peggy you will never be forgotten"!

I took early retirement at the age of fifty-eight, whilst I still had energy to do the things I always wanted to do. No more sick notes for the employer or having to ask for leave to go and visit my far-flung family and friends.

Because of my lifelong interest in nursing, I attended the Elizabeth Thomas Seminar in Nottingham in November, although at this time I had no intention of returning to practice. These seminars were run primarily by volunteers so I did not mind getting involved.

Having said that, in January 2011 I joined the National Health Service Professionals (NHSP) as an agency nurse. This would allow me to work on a flexible basis at the Nottingham University Hospitals NHS Trust.

Returning to work in this way would help me keep my brain active and continue to help wherever I was needed. I enjoyed the fact that this would be on my terms however.

In November 2011, for black history month, I was asked to attend a meeting at the East Midlands office of the RCN and give a presentation, focusing on diversity and human rights - discussing how employers deal with employees from different backgrounds. I put a Power Point presentation together on respecting different cultures. I gave examples of how it can have a great impact on people's lives in some instances – such as issues surrounding food or how to support staff who are ill. It generated a lot of discussion about famous people and prominent leaders who helped to abolish slavery as well as appreciating nursing today in our ethnic diverse world. It was quite an entertaining day to say the least, and while a sensitive subject, we all ended up laughing several times. I repeated the presentation in December at the request of the RCN.

I was asked later on to do another Power Point Presentation on common eye problems to Practice Nurses. This time I was paid by the drug company Novartis. The practice nurses were very pleased and contacted me for advice when needed.

In December I attended mandatory training on safeguarding vulnerable children and adults. NHS Professionals expect all their registered nurses to complete the mandatory courses in order to fulfill their practice requirements.

At the end of March 2013, Nelson and I went to Zambia after Nelson's elder sister Elinah Mwando lost her daughter Rebecca. She had already lost four sons:

Jimmy, Sailas, Louis, and Nelson (nephew). We visited their home town of Mumbwa, and went to the cemetery where they were all buried. This visit gave us the opportunity to visit the graves of my elder brother Stanley Sankeni Yikona who was buried in Mwinilunga, (who had died the previous year) and my niece Peggy Kanombe, in Kitwe, who had died after our visit in 2010 as previously mentioned.

To lose an extended family member, as opposed to a primary one, is still very painful to us as we are a united family. Coping with death can be very difficult, but at the same time we comfort one another. In our Zambian culture, despite the time it may take, our values compel us to visit the families of the bereaved. During our time of grief, we were blessed with another grandson, so throughout our pain, joy found us again. We were thankful for this event and from September to October we went to the USA to babysit our grandson Adonis (my late brothers' daughters' child).

Both in 2014 and 2015 I have been involved in Diaspora (defined as anyone living away from their country of origin or ancestral homeland). We are the Zambian Diaspora. I was appointed Chairperson of the Zambian Diaspora Initiative for Health, working closely with the Zambian High Commission in London, and for a short time I worked as a UK co-ordinator on a maternity leave cover.

My first presentation was to a varied group of people, including trade professionals and those involved in health matters. My topic was 'Nursing at Home and Abroad' The second presentation was entitled 'Harnessing the Diaspora Experience'. This aimed to encourage Zambian health-care professionals here, to utilise their skills which then can be used to support peoples back home - such as when I used my own initiative and resources to collect and deliver the nursing and medical books to Zambia. For me, 'just sending money' is not enough.

In 2016, I visited Zambian schools again with my husband Nelson and Peggy Katambi, a colleague who works in Derby. As before, we collected medical books and journals and other educational equipment and distributed them. Nelson also took football kits, footballs and air pumps to Chipapa Primary School, the school he attended as a boy.

Changes in Healthcare Provision and Developments

The introduction of new standards and codes of practice worldwide have contributed to how healthcare is provided, and the standards that are expected. There are now intensive training programmes based on scientific understanding and knowledge, where once, traditional methods were passed down from generation to generation.

Change of uniform policies and style of dress have evolved to help make nurses more approachable and relevant to modern life, and modern life has changed completely. Advancements in technology, healthcare and communication across the world both reduce and elevate us all to the same level. Florence Nightingale and Mary Seacole, nursing pioneers, worked in very different situations and contexts in comparison to us. While tremendous changes have occurred since, one thing remains the same across nursing: the dedication a nursing individual has for his/her patients.

Despite who you are and what you do, life is precious, and it should be enjoyed for as long as possible. Enjoying life is an aid to keeping fit and healthy. I now work only part-time. I have the best of both worlds. I can choose whether to work or not. I look at this as a license to freedom of movement, freedom from stress and timetables.

I can spend time with the next generation. The same as a lot of grandparents, I would say my grandchildren are more enjoyable than my children. This is because I have time to enjoy them! Furthermore, when you have spoilt them by over-feeding them with sweets, chips and burgers, and run them around until they drop, I can give them back!

Retirement can lead to loneliness, depression and illness. But I am very fortunate. I have found that the secret to my happy 'retirement' is to keep busy, keep in touch with friends and relatives and keep active.

Finally, I chose to publish this book in August 2018 as I have had some memorable times in my life in this month:

24th August 1997 - my father Dryden Samonu Yikona passed away

31st August 2003 - my mother Fonisiya Yihemba Yikona passed away

16th August 1991 - I commenced work at the QMC

16th August 2010 - I retired from full-time work in the NHS

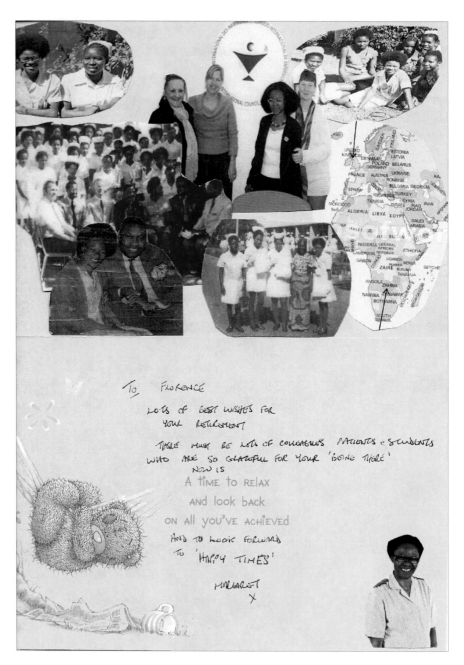

To FLORENCE

LOTS OF BEST WISHES FOR
YOUR RETIREMENT

THERE MUST BE LOTS OF COLLEAGUES, PATIENTS & STUDENTS
WHO ARE SO GRATEFUL FOR YOUR 'BEING THERE'
NOW IS
A time to RELAX
And look back
ON All you've Achieved
AND TO LOOK FORWARD
TO 'HAPPY TIMES'

MARGARET
X

From colleague Margaret Harman

Appendix 1 - 'How People See Me' - Contributions from families and friends for the use in this book

A questionnaire was distributed to a diverse group to see how they see me. The following graphs and pie charts are the results of the questionnaire.

Sample Identification (n=35)

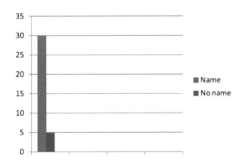

Ethnicity

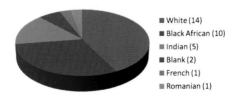

How long have you known Benoni?

- 1-5 years
- 6-11 years
- 12-20 years
- >20 years

In what capacity have you known Benoni?

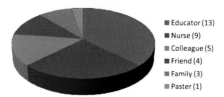

- Educator (13)
- Nurse (9)
- Colleague (5)
- Friend (4)
- Family (3)
- Paster (1)

Give a short account of Benoni in your own words

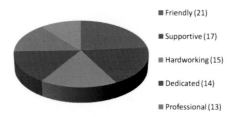

- Friendly (21)
- Supportive (17)
- Hardworking (15)
- Dedicated (14)
- Professional (13)

Appendix 1 - 'How People See Me' - Contributions from families and friends for the use in this book

Nelson Mwando

I was a former footballer in the 1970's, where I was fortunate to play alongside Florence's late older brother, Richard Yikona. I remember giving Richard many lifts to and from the University and going to social events together, we became good friends. As a sports man my priority was the game, little did I know that my friendship with Richard would lead to the meeting of my future wife, Richards's sister Florence Benoni Kakunu Yikona.

'76 was the year that I truly saw Florence, walking towards Ridgeway. I drove alongside her as she happily ignored me, but as an honest man, I gave her a lift. This was the beginning of our lifelong friendship and relationship as husband and wife.

Both Mwando and Yikona families accepted each other, we became one. Florence got on very well with my late brother David and shared many secrets of my childhood. David always told me to not disappoint my wife and her parents.

In the early 80's I was best man and chauffer to the eldest daughter Gertrude of late Mr. William Kadimba and Mrs. Edith Kadimba. Dr. Daka, (I had already met Mr. Daka at Munali Secondary School in Zambia) was to marry Gertrude. The wedding was beautiful to say the least; Florence remained in Lusaka to look after our 3 month old son Samonu. My late father-in-law wrote a kind letter, referring to me as one of his best sons-in-law and how we should obey and respect each other. As a husband, I am truly grateful for the acceptance of my in laws: late Mr. William Kadimba and Mrs. Kadimba; late father-in-law Mr. Dryden Yikona and late mother-in-law Mrs. Fonisiya Yihemba Yikona.

I come from a very small family; Florence has a large and extended family that I cherish dearly. I love my uncles, nephews, nieces, cousins, brothers, sisters, children and friends. I was taught to always respect and treat my-in-laws as my own.

Education and faith are crucial in any relationship. I will always support my wife in her studies and practices as an immigrant nurse. Our relationship has produced four beautiful children and the raising of a brilliant nephew who is our youngest son, Mambwe Chintu, my late sister-in-law Abigail Chintu's son, who trusted me to raise him. Mambwe's late father, Humphrey Chintu, became a good younger brother in marriage and we shared future business ideas together. May their souls rest in peace.

My wife is faithful and unbreakable. She is an educator, traveler, colleague, mother and friend. I will always remember to be a wise husband to win credibility for life.

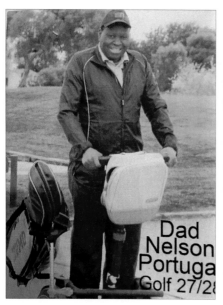

Dad
Nelson
Portuga
Golf 27/2

Appendix 1 - 'How People See Me' - Contributions from families and friends for the use in this book

Sailas Mwando Mwando, first born son

Mum is the reason I am standing and prospering today. She has never given up or lost faith in who I would become. She has helped me to succeed. Mum has been there by my side no matter what. Through my trials and tribulations she has encouraged me to find myself and know who I am, to know that I am worthy of respect and love.

She is truly the greatest woman and mother.

Evah Mwando & Lydia Okubote

Our mother is intelligent, generous and the most incredible woman we know. She is the reason we are who we are. She has allowed us to flourish and succeed in every single way.

Remembering moments like graduation. We ran from one end of the University to the other to hand in a dissertation, with mum right by our side. Mum organised joint graduation parties, with family and friends to celebrate our achievements. A kind hearted soul who will do anything for the people she loves.

Mum puts others first without complaint. She sees the best in all of us and truly believes in our potential and will not give up until that potential is reached.

In honour of my mum, my (Lydia) first born daughter is named Talia Florence Abigail Omatayo Okubote, born on 24th August.

Mum is truly one of a kind.

Appendix 1 - 'How People See Me' - Contributions from families and friends for the use in this book

Corinna Hoptroff

I have known Florence for approximately 25 years when she worked as Staff Nurse and Sister in the Nottingham Queen's Medical Centre Eye Clinic. I was the Ophthalmic tutor in the School of Nursing and we would liaise regarding the education and training of all student nurses passing through the department. Florence was extremely supportive of the students and created learning opportunities for them in all of the Ophthalmic departments. We would meet regularly and I felt very supported by her interest and enthusiasm. During this time Florence became a good friend. Always sympathetic and understanding she continues to give her full support to me and my family. She has a great sense of humour and I will not forget one occasion when she telephoned the School of Nursing to speak to me. The receptionist asked what department she worked in and Florence replied "Eye Clinic" but because of her accent this was mistaken for "Night Cleaner". After some delay I realised what had happened, and was actually quite reluctant to tell Florence about the note I had received from the receptionist as I didn't want to offend her. But something told me she would find it funny, and she did, understanding the joke fully, laughing long and hard and often reminding me of the event! I am so pleased to hear that Florence is producing a book as she will be honest and thorough, and this will be a very interesting addition to the autobiographical world.

Appendix 1 - 'How People See Me' - Contributions from families and friends for the use in this book

Permission to use NUH/QMC photographs from Neal Hughes.

Neal Hughes

Senior Corporate Designer, Communications Team,
University Hospital NHS Trust, Queen's Medical Centre, Nottingham.

I can confirm, by written form of this email, that I give full permission to Florence Mwando to use my name and associated information in her book.

I've known Florence for many years and knew her through friends who worked in the Eye Department at Nottingham University Hospitals NHS Trust. She was an absolute credit to the department, the Trust and nursing in general, with her warmth and compassion for her patients, their families and colleagues alike. I photographed Florence on many occasions, either for general PR work or because I needed a helpful nurse. I of course returned these favours whenever possible to help Florence illustrate whatever projects she had on the go at that time. It was always good fun working with Florence and incredibly interesting. She has literally forgotten more about ophthalmological nursing than some people will ever know. She was and always will be a huge source of inspiration and kindness and I feel incredibly lucky to have worked with her and to be able to fondly call her a friend.

Appendix 1 - 'How People See Me' - Contributions from families and friends for the use in this book

Christine Jago

Admissions Officer, Ophthalmology Department, QMC (Retired)

The first time I met Florence in Eye Clinic Reception at the QMC, she mistook me for my sister, Sue Ashby. After I had forgiven her we became firm friends and I was able to offer her assistance with various projects producing teaching packages, helping with the preparation of study days and a Head & Neck Study Day, meeting and escorting the guest speaker and his dog from and to the railway station. Considering that guide dogs are essential, it is however appreciated that additional care is crucial in ensuring the visually impaired board the right train, and are safely on the right platform.

Florence is kind, considerate and always willing to help others. She is generous to a fault in every way, and totally committed to improving the lot of as many people as she can.

Her life, career and family are in England, but she is always grateful to her country of origin, Zambia, for giving her the education and opportunity to go further.

She is totally focused on family, both immediate and extended, which shows in her lovely children who are a testament to her love.

Appendix 1 - 'How People See Me' - Contributions from families and friends for the use in this book

Questionnaire FBK Mwando

Name (optional)........ *Keith Knox*

Ethnicity........ *White, British*

How long have you known Benoni? 1-5 years...... 6 – 11 years...... (12 – 20 years).... over 20 years.......

In what capacity do you know Benoni? (Friend....) (Colleague...) (Nurse.).... Educator....... Mother.......

Give a short account of Benoni in your own words (keep it brief and polite please)

I've known Benoni since the early 1990's. Firstly, when I first met her I couldn't believe how old she was, she looked so young! And I might add, she still does. So much energy too! Very difficult to hold her back, so much enthusiasm. Benoni, during the time that I worked with her, was a great colleague and an enduring source of support and encouragement, always saying "oh no, you can do this and you can do that," always positive. My son William died after a short illness in 1998, aged 3 years. During his illness he was in hospital for a time and Benoni gave her time unselfishly helping to work and care for him. After his death I found it difficult

DATE COMPLETED:

to travel, becoming very anxious about any journey away from my family. During this time I reluctantly took a flight to Glasgow with Benoni on a work trip. The flight there was ok and sitting next to Benoni I kept control of my inner anxiety and we arrived in Glasgow without incident. However, the planned flight back was a different story. Suffice to say I got 'spooked' by the announcement that the flight would be delayed due to a technical fault and when we eventually boarded the plane I became more anxious and agitated because I did not have a seat next to Benoni. There was a short exchange with some other passengers on the plane during which I thought to myself "That's it, I'm getting off!" I promptly stood up and proceeded quickly down the isle of the plane and walked off the plane. I could hear the stewardess saying "We'll find you seats together", but by then it was too late, my mind was made up. I have a lasting memory of Benoni shouting protestations at the crew as she left the plane after me. So there we were stranded in Glasgow. However, Benoni, as ever resourceful, came up with a plan for us to get a bus to Edinburgh to stay with her cousin; relatives everywhere! We did go to Edinburgh and we eventually found her cousin's flat and stayed the night. I slept while Benoni and her cousin discussed, I think with some laughter, the events of the day. I say we stayed the night, this was no more than 6 hours as we were soon back on a coach to Glasgow airport where with the help of kind airport staff we boarded a plane, which we stayed on, back to Nottingham. I think this story is now part of the folklore associated with Benoni's family... When I meet members of Benoni's family they always laugh and warmly welcome me like a long lost brother and I know they are thinking of the aeroplane adventure! Thankfully, I have flown several times since then and have not felt inclined to get off the plane! They do say that time is a great healer.

Benoni is one of the most generous people I have ever known, filled with youthful energy and a heart so big she could, I think, support the whole world.

Completed   19 . 2 . 2016.

Appendix 1 - 'How People See Me' - Contributions from families and friends for the use in this book

Name (optional) *Helen Knox*

Ethnicity *White British*

How long have you known Benoni? 1-5 years...... 6 – 11 years...... 12 – 20 years ✓ over 20 years......

In what capacity do you know Benoni? Friend ✓ Colleague...... Nurse...... Educator...... Mother......

Give a short account of Benoni in your own words (keep it brief and polite please)

Florence has been a good friend to our whole family for many years and has always been quick to offer support and help in times of need. I especially always remember how kind she was when our eldest son then aged 3 was in hospital not long before he died. I was staying in hospital with William and Florence would arrive early on the ward before her shift started and would help me wash and care for him. I really appreciated her help and kind words and cheerfulness at that difficult time.

Florence has also taken care of my husband when they have attended conferences together and he has had difficulties with travelling and organising himself! She also takes an interest in our children and offered our son much encouragement when she bumped into him when he was on work experience at QMC.

DATE COMPLETED:

19/2/16

76

Appendix 1 - 'How People See Me' - Contributions from families and friends for the use in this book

Name (optional)........ Shikha Sud ....

Ethnicity...

How long have you known Benoni? 1-5 years...... 6 – 11 years...... 12 – 20 years... (over 20 years..)....

In what capacity do you know Benoni? (Friend....) (Colleague..)... Nurse....... Educator....... Mother.......

Give a short account of Benoni in your own words (keep it brief and polite please)

Benoni is a loyal friend who can be relied on at any time. She is warm - hearted and kind.
She is a dedicated nurse and she makes it her mission to not only help those immediately around her, but also to educate and empower nurses internationally to deliver excellent healthcare to those who need it.
Benoni is truly an amazing person who inspires and encourages everyone to achieve their goals in life.

Appendix 1 - 'How People See Me' - Contributions from families and friends for the use in this book

Questionnaire FBK Mwando

Name (optional) Mazz Eles

Ethnicity...... BRITISH -

How long have you known Benoni? 1-5 years.✓.. 6 – 11 years...... 12 – 20 years... over 20 years......

In what capacity do you know Benoni? Friend.✓... Colleague..✓.... Nurse....... Educator....... Mother.......
CONFIDANT

Give a short account of Benoni in your own words (keep it brief and polite please)

FLORENCE INITIALLY A COLLEAGUE BECAME A TRUSTED FRIEND. REMEMBER SPENDING TIME /HOURS ON DOING EXCEL WITH LOTS OF LAUGHS. AND SHARING SPECIAL TIMES.

A TRUSTED FRIEND WHO FEELS YOUR PAIN, SHARES YOUR EMOTIONS AND MAKES YOU LAUGH ;).

SHE'S AN INSPIRATION, SURVIVOR AND HOLDS HER GROUND BOTH ETHICALLY & MORALLY LEAVING A PERMANENT SATISFYING IMPRESSION THAT MAKES FLORENCE,.. FLORENCE.

MUCH LOVE WITH GREATEST RESPECT.

DATE COMPLETED : 8.3.16 ;)

Appendix 1 - 'How People See Me' - Contributions from families and friends for the use in this book

Questionnaire FBK Mwando

Name (optional)........ Aniwe ....

Ethnicity........ African. ....

How long have you known Benoni? 1-5 years...... 6 – 11 years...... 12 – 20 years... over 20 years.......

In what capacity do you know Benoni? Friend..✓.... Colleague....... Nurse..✓.. Educator......✓... Mother....✓...

Give a short account of Benoni in your own words (keep it brief and polite please)

Florence is a mother, a nurse, a sister, a wife, educator and above all a great friend. All you need to say is I need help and she will be by your side in no time. Most of the times you don't even have to ask because she knows and senses your my needs!

Appendix 1 - 'How People See Me' - Contributions from families and friends for the use in this book

Questionnaire FBK Mwando

Name (optional)...... KATHRYN WILLBOND

Ethnicity.... BRITISH

How long have you known Benoni? 1-5 years...... 6 – 11 years...... 12 – 20 years... (over 20 years.....).

In what capacity do you know Benoni? (Friend).... (Colleague).... (Nurse)... (Educator)... (Mother)...

Give a short account of Benoni in your own words (keep it brief and polite please)

Florence has always been a very good guide and leader.
Florence is a nurse whom I look up to and admire
very much.
A very good teacher. I have always respected Florence.
I have watched Florence over the years, she has
remained the same nurse, good, kind person.
I regard Florence as a true friend as well as
a colleague.

DATE COMPLETED:
13. 1. 16.

Appendix 1 - 'How People See Me' - Contributions from families and friends for the use in this book

Benoni is a dedicated and hard-working individual who cares about just everyone. Friendly and approachable it is easy to relate to Benoni and hard not to love admire her caring and nurturing personality. Despite facing several challenges and having numerous "things on her plate," Benoni has been able to work hard and achieve her many highly honourable goals & in life!

Florence is an exceptional individual, both in her nursing capacity and in her commitment to colleagues and the advancement of nursing education. In 2009 I assisted Florence in organising the 21st Century Head & Neck Conference which thanks to her efforts was a resounding success. Florence gives 110% in everything she does.

Florence has been always a support and teacher to me. Florence has had a good impact on my Career. I have huge respect for her and see her as my role model. To work with Florence has always been my pleasure. I see Florence as my friend and colleague. Florene Mwando is our II nd Florence Nightingale. That's for sure!

Appendix 1 - 'How People See Me' - Contributions from families and friends for the use in this book

Name (optional) Amie Mandang

Ethnicity BLACK AFRICAN

How long have you known Benoni? 1-5 years...... 6 – 11 years..... (12 – 20 years).. over 20 years.......

In what capacity do you know Benoni? (Friend)..... (Colleague)...... (Nurse)...... (Educator)...... Mother.......

Give a short account of Benoni in your own words (keep it brief and polite please)

I first met Benoni in 2001 when l was doing a post graduate teaching course at The University of Nottingham. Since then, she has supported, guided and assisted me in all sorts of ways. She is a very kind individual and is very passionate about nursing. Her professionalism always shines through whatever she is involved in. I wish her the very best with the first edition of her book.

She is a lovely lady, very professional, Her knowledge is variable and very vast.
She is a hard worker and is very well like by patients and work colleagues.

Appendix 1 - 'How People See Me' - Contributions from families and friends for the use in this book

Name (optional)...... Katherine Rocke

Ethnicity........ White British

How long have you known Benoni? (1-5 years.).... 6 – 11 years...... 12 – 20 years... over 20 years......

In what capacity do you know Benoni? Friend....... (Colleague)... (Nurse.)..... Educator....... Mother.......

Give a short account of Benoni in your own words (keep it brief and polite please)

Florence is an inspiration! Her Commitment to nursing, both in the UK and internationally is to be recommended. I have met Florence as she works agency shifts around her many other commitments, and have a huge respect for her firstly as a nurse and secondly as a leader. I hope that the nurses on my ward take note of her example, as I think we rarely come across people like her who give so much of themselves.

She is very professional and helpful. Always keen to teach to students and newly qualified nurses. She always approach patients and staff very professionaly. Very good person, nurse and educator.

Appendix 1 - 'How People See Me' - Contributions from families and friends for the use in this book

I know Mwando, named as florence as a Customer to my business; and later as a next street lady which later hapenned to be a friend; nurse; educator and a very good mother. she is very friendly; Co-operative and a very good human being. she is really always there for me, my husband and my son whom we are very comfortable; reliable and trustworthy. we love her and her family & let god bless her & family

Rohini chandu Rohan
we love

Florence (Benoni) has always been intellectually inquisitive with an enquiring mind. She is diligent & dedicated in all her endeavours without losing her compassion so essential in her chosen field of work.

Appendix 1 - How People See Me

Questionnaire FBK Mwando

Name (optional)...... Deborran Hughes ....

Ethnicity........ White British ....

How long have you known Benoni? (1-5 years...)... 6 – 11 years...... 12 – 20 years... over 20 years.......

In what capacity do you know Benoni? Friend....... Colleague...... (Nurse.).... (Educator.....) Mother.......

Give a short account of Benoni in your own words (keep it brief and polite please)

I first met Benoni as a student nurse and was impressed how she put a learning package together for pupils under wing. She was also very knowledgable within her working area and ensured that students were incorporated into the daily running of the ward areas. She organised ensight visits into the widespread path of opthalmology, making the placement variable.

Benoni is a very hard working & compassionate person, always has a smile for everyone.
It's a pleasure to call her my friend/colleague.

85

Appendix 1 - 'How People See Me' - Contributions from families and friends for the use in this book

University Hospitals of Leicester **NHS**
NHS Trust

Caring at its best

Department of Ophthalmology
Leicester Royal Infirmary
Leicester LE1 5WW

8 May 2018

I have known Florence Mwando as a professional colleague for over 20 years. We previously worked together in the Ophthalmology Department of Nottingham University Hospitals.

She brought an enthusiastic and proactive approach to the modernisation of the profession of ophthalmic nursing at the hospital.
Training and education was greatly improved by her introduction of structure and quality to the teaching programme for both existing and new staff.

She also extended and developed the roles of qualified ophthalmic nurses by creating the opportunity for increased clinical responsibility and with a resultant increase in clinic capacity for patient assessment and treatment in this busy NHS department.

Much of this was achieved by her careful and persistent liaison between all the professions working within the Ophthalmology Department – nurses, optometrists, orthoptists and ophthalmologists.
By successful 'building of bridges' between the professions, trust was developed in turn resulting in improving confidence in the expanding role of the ophthalmic nurse.

M P Rubinstein PhD FCOptom

Clinical Lead Optometrist   Leicester Royal Infirmary   Leicester
Honorary Professor   School of Life and Health Sciences   Aston University   Birmingham

Appendix 1 - 'How People See Me' - Contributions from families and friends for the use in this book

Questionnaire FBK Mwando

Name (optional)...DR. I. K. HEBBAR...

Ethnicity...British (Asian British)...

How long have you known Benoni? 1-5 years...... 6 – 11 years...... 12 – 20 years... (over 20 years...)...

In what capacity do you know Benoni? Friend...✓... Colleague....... Nurse...✓... Educator....... Mother.......

Give a short account of Benoni in your own words (keep it brief and polite please)

Benoni is an honest, hard working, very reliable, extremely helpful and caring person.

29/4/18.

Appendix 1 - 'How People See Me' - Contributions from families and friends for the use in this book

Questionnaire FBK Mwando

Name (optional)...

Ethnicity... British ....

How long have you known Benoni? 1-5 years...... 6 – 11 years...... 12 – 20 years(.. over 20 years......

In what capacity do you know Benoni? (Friend...). (Colleague...). (Nurse)... (Educator)..... Mother......

Give a short account of Benoni in your own words (keep it brief and polite please)

I worked with.. Benoni initially as a student ophthalmic nurse. She was an excellent. teacher and very conscientious. Benoni also encouraged me to join IONA INTERNATIONAL OPHTHALMIC NURSES ASSOCIATION. We have been on several ophthalmic study todays together. Benoni also helped and encouraged me to give a presentation to other ophthalmic staff on a cataract research study at Nottingham University Hospital.

Appendix 1 - 'How People See Me' - Contributions from families and friends for the use in this book

Questionnaire FBK Mwando

Name (optional)...

Ethnicity........... Black African ....

How long have you known Benoni? 1-5 years...... 6 – 11 years...... 12 – 20 years... over 20 years.......

In what capacity do you know Benoni? Friend... Colleague... Nurse... Educator... Mother......

Give a short account of Benoni in your own words (keep it brief and polite please)

I have known Florence for a long time. She is very hard working and always puts patients at the centre of actions.

She is an excellent teacher who participated in the development of nursing pathways for AMD, from when PDT was introduced through to the introduction of anti-VEGF therapies. This is in addition to pioneering nurse-led and delivered fluorescein angiography services in Nottingham.

She supported the University tutors to develop the Ophthalmic Nurse Training Programme in the Nottingham School of Nursing.

She is an excellent mother. I've met all her children!

Appendix 1 - 'How People See Me' - Contributions from families and friends for the use in this book

Questionnaire FBK Mwando

Name (optional)....Lexshmi....Lynn..

Ethnicity......Mixed - other (British)................................

How long have you known Benoni? 1-5 years...... (6 – 11 years.)... 12 – 20 years... over 20 years.......

In what capacity do you know Benoni? Friend..✓.. Colleague..✓.. Nurse..✓.. Educator..✓.. Mother..✓..

Give a short account of Benoni in your own words (keep it brief and polite please)

I first met Benoni on my first day as a student nurse at Nottingham University hospitals. As a result of this experience, at Benoni's side, I became the nurse I am today supporting my staff & patients as a practice development matron.

Throughout my placement & at our meetings ever since, I have found Benoni to be a truely inspiring person. Her passion for nursing (and life) has motivated me throughout my career.

Thank you to a great friend & colleague.

Benoni is polite and proffessional. Caring and helps others. She goes out her way to help you. As my Educator too she learnt me a lot whilst on a placement within her unit.

90

Appendix 1 - 'How People See Me' - Contributions from families and friends for the use in this book

Questionnaire FBK Mwando

Name (optional)........ JOAN HAMILTON .... SRN ONI)

Ethnicity........ CAUCASION .... BRITISH.

How long have you known Benoni? 1-5 years...... 6 – 11 years...... 12 – 20 years... over 20 years....25 years

In what capacity do you know Benoni? Friend...✓... Colleague...✓.... Nurse..✓... Educator..✓... Mother.......

Give a short account of Benoni in your own words (keep it brief and polite please)

Appearanc) at first meeting with lots of potential and has proved herself over the years.
Very heapful a good teacher
A lovely friend

Joan Hamilton

Benoni was my first Mentor in Nursing on my first placement, If it was not for her encorgement I would not be where I am today debty Sister in A+E! Thank you.

Amy-laite Het.

Appendix 1 - 'How People See Me' - Contributions from families and friends for the use in this book

Questionnaire FBK Mwando

Name (optional)..

Ethnicity..Mauritian   British..

How long have you known Benoni? 1-5 years...... 6 – 11 years...... 12 – 20 years... over 20 years.......

In what capacity do you know Benoni? Friend....... Colleague....... Nurse....... Educator....... Mother.......

Give a short account of Benoni in your own words (keep it brief and polite please)

I have known Benoni first as a professional and then as a friend. she has a cheerful personality and well known teacher at QMCH Hospital. she persuaded me to join the International ophthalmic Association and was the backbone of the society for a long time - she has good organising and communications skills. she is patient, optimistic and responsible person. In the lord she trust.

J Jeeavoo JJ

92

Appendix 1 - 'How People See Me' - Contributions from families and friends for the use in this book

Questionnaire FBK Mwando

Name (optional) *PASTOR NIGEL YATES*

Ethnicity *BRITISH*

How long have you known Benoni? 1-5 years...... 6 – 11 years...... 12 – 20 years... over 20 years ✓

In what capacity do you know Benoni? Friend ✓ Colleague....... Nurse....... Educator....... Mother......

Give a short account of Benoni in your own words (keep it brief and polite please)

I HAVE KNOWN BENONI .... FLORENCE .... FOR 21½ YEARS AS PASTOR OF THE OASIS CHRISTIAN CENTRE, BEESTON . SHE IS A WONDERFUL, ENERGETIC, STRONG, FAITHFUL, FAITH FULL, HARD WORKING, WELCOMING ENCOURAGING, INTELLIGENT, SMILING, THOUGHTFUL, CARING, LOVING, DETERMINED, EDUCATED, KNOWLEDGEABLE, UNDERSTANDING, HELPFUL, FAMILY LOVING, SPIRITUAL MOTHER, ... LADY HER VISION TO MENTOR NURSES IS LEGENDARY. MY LIFE HAS BEEN ENHANCED IMMENSELY BY KNOWING HER .

N. Yates

DATE COMPLETED: 22/2/16

Appendix 1 - 'How People See Me' - Contributions from families and friends for the use in this book

Questionnaire FBK Mwando

Name (optional).......... DR JOSEPH YIKONA ....

Ethnicity.......... Black African ....

How long have you known Benoni? 1-5 years...... 6 – 11 years...... 12 – 20 years... over 20 years... X

In what capacity do you know Benoni? Friend....... Colleague....... Nurse....... Educator....... Mother.......
Older Sister

Give a short account of Benoni in your own words (keep it brief and polite please)

I stand today as a Consultant Physician ~~with~~
following a priceless Contribution to my upbringing by
Florence. A true Contributor to the adage "it takes a villag
to bring up a child".

~~If I did more~~

Had I done more listening, may be I would have
changed the world. Alas, hopefully I change some patien
lives.

Yikona
/ 10 /march/2018.

Appendix 1 - 'How People See Me' - Contributions from families and friends for the use in this book

Questionnaire FBK Mwando

Name (optional)...... *Tionge Tihona*

Ethnicity...... *African*

How long have you known Benoni? 1-5 years...... 6 – 11 years...... (12 – 20 years...) over 20 years.......

In what capacity do you know Benoni? Friend....... Colleague....... Nurse....... Educator....... Mother...... (Auntie)

Give a short account of Benoni in your own words (keep it brief and polite please)

Auntie has always been like a second MUM. She always calls to check up on us with the kindest of thoughts. Wouldn't trade her for the world. Auntie puts everyone first even if she is having a tough time.

Appendix 1 - 'How People See Me' - Contributions from families and friends for the use in this book

Name (optional)............ MAUREEN BURROWS ....

Ethnicity............ WHITE BRITISH ....

How long have you known Benoni? 1-5 years...... 6 – 11 years...... 12 – 20 years... over 20 years.✓...

In what capacity do you know Benoni? Friend..✓... Colleague....... Nurse.✓... Educator.✓... Mother.✓...

Give a short account of Benoni in your own words (keep it brief and polite please)

- Benoni is a true friend. As a friend she is always there, caring; truthful and compassionate. She always goes the extra mile if needed, as she does with all aspects of her life.

- As a nurse Benoni is knowledgable and empathetic and she uses her full range of skills in order to assess and treat her patients.

- Benoni is a excellent educator in her field. Her up-to-date research-based knowledge is unsurpassed and her teaching skills are something to be envied-due to her knowledge and her ability to impart that knowledge.

- Benoni's children; her extended family; her friends who she treats as a member of her family will all tell you what a wonderful mother she is.

DATE COMPLETED:

21st January 2016.

Appendix 1 - 'How People See Me' - Contributions from families and friends for the use in this book

Name (optional).............Harminder S Aua........................

Ethnicity.........Asian (Indian)...

How long have you known Benoni? 1-5 years...... 6 – 11 years...... 12 – 20 years... over 20 years.......

In what capacity do you know Benoni? Friend....... Colleague...... Nurse...... Educator...... Mother.......

Give a short account of Benoni in your own words (keep it brief and polite please)

Benoni has been a very motivated, committed and dedicated individual who has driven innovation in her profession and always worked and contributed well beyond her contractual obligations.

HSAua

14/7/16

97

Appendix 1 - 'How People See Me' - Contributions from families and friends for the use in this book

Name (optional) JENNIFER ANNE DOOHAN

Ethnicity BRITISH.

How long have you known Benoni? 1-5 years...... 6 – 11 years...... 12 – 20 years...... over 20 years.......

In what capacity do you know Benoni? Friend.✓.. Colleague.✓... Nurse.✓.... Educator.✓.... Mother.......

Give a short account of Benoni in your own words (keep it brief and polite please)

Dedicated professional nurse and very compassionate and caring, very patient focussed, helpful to those in need, selfless, truly believes in good in people and always there to help.

Give a short account of Benoni in your own words (keep it brief and polite please)

I worked with Benoni for several years as a colleague in ophthalmology. Throughout this time she was a committed and enthusiastic member of staff. She was an inspiration to colleagues, learners and students It was a pleasure to know her.

Appendix 2 - Yikona Family Tree

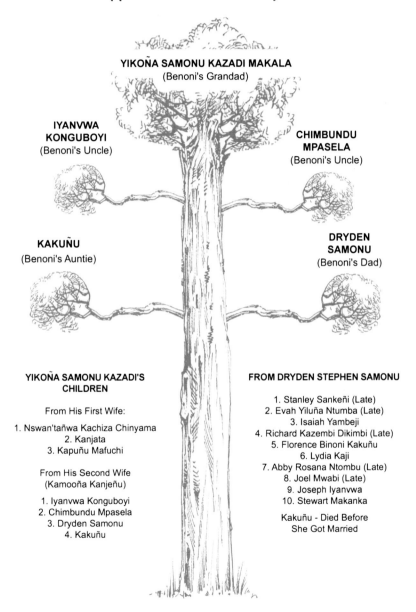

YIKOÑA SAMONU KAZADI MAKALA
(Benoni's Grandad)

IYANVWA KONGUBOYI
(Benoni's Uncle)

CHIMBUNDU MPASELA
(Benoni's Uncle)

KAKUÑU
(Benoni's Auntie)

DRYDEN SAMONU
(Benoni's Dad)

YIKOÑA SAMONU KAZADI'S CHILDREN

From His First Wife:

1. Nswan'tañwa Kachiza Chinyama
2. Kanjata
3. Kapuñu Mafuchi

From His Second Wife
(Kamooña Kanjeñu)

1. Iyanvwa Konguboyi
2. Chimbundu Mpasela
3. Dryden Samonu
4. Kakuñu

FROM DRYDEN STEPHEN SAMONU

1. Stanley Sankeñi (Late)
2. Evah Yiluña Ntumba (Late)
3. Isaiah Yambeji
4. Richard Kazembi Dikimbi (Late)
5. Florence Binoni Kakuñu
6. Lydia Kaji
7. Abby Rosana Ntombu (Late)
8. Joel Mwabi (Late)
9. Joseph Iyanvwa
10. Stewart Makanka

Kakuñu - Died Before
She Got Married

Photographs

Glossary

Aeroplane = Ndeki.

Appreciate = Kusakilila.

Are you alright? = Mwakola.

Auntie = Tata Wamumbanda/muhela atata.

Author = nsoneki.

Beautiful = lubanji.

Blind = kufwa mensu.

Bye bye = wawawa.

Cheers = chinawahi.

Colleague = mukwawu / mukwetu.

Cousin = musonyi/musonyindi.

Dangerous = Chafwana.

Diversity awareness = Kwiluka yuma Yamboka.

Elderly person = mukulumpi.

Establishing = kushimatisha.

Eyes = mensu.

Friend = ibwambu.

God = Nzambi.

Happy = kuzang'alala.

House = itala.

How are you? = mudi ng'ahi?

Husband = Iyala Wasumbula.

Immigrant Nurse = Nansi kumatung'a acheng'i.

Malaria = mashika/malaria.

Medicine = Yitumbu.

Polite = Kavumbi.

Retire = Kukumisha Nyidimu.

Rude = Kasawuntu.

Sad = kuneng'a.

Shelter = Chota.

Shivering = kuzaala.

Sickness = Kukata.

Slow but sure = Wada chovu wekuta.

Sore = chilonda.

Study = kutang'a.

Study = kutang'a.

Train = Masuwa.

Traveller = mukwakwenda.

Uncle = mandumi.

United family = chisaka chadinung'a.

Wealth of life = iheta dawumi.

Welcome = Shikenu/kushikija.

Wife & mother = Wasumbuka, wukweti anyana.

Work hard = Kuzata nang'ovu.

Young person = Kansi.

References

Anionwu, E.N. (2005) A Short History of Mary Seacole a resource of nurses and students. London: Royal College of Nursing

"Charles R. Swindoll Quotes." BrainyQuote.com. Xplore Inc, 2018 23 July 2018. https://www.brainyquote.com/quotes/charles_r_swindoll_38832

Halpern, D. and Cheung, F. (2008) Women at the Top. Powerful Leaders Tell Us How to Combine Work and Family. United Kingdom: A John Wiley & Sons, Ltd, Publication

Holy Bible, New International Version, 1984. London: International Bible Society/Hodder & Stoughton

Nursing and Midwifery Council. (2006) Standards to Support Learning and Assessment in Parctice: NMC Standards for Mentors, Practice Teachers and Teachers. London: Nursing and Midwifery Council

"Og Mandino Quotes." BrainyQuote.com. Xplore Inc, 2018. 23 July 2018. http://www.brainyquote.com/quotes/og_mandino_157864

The New Testiment of Our Lord and Savior Jesus Christ, revised standard version, 1971. New York: American Bible Society.

"Winston Churchill Quotes." BrainyQuote.com. Xplore Inc, 2018. 23 July 2018. http://www.brainyquote.com/quotes/Winston_churchill_131192

Acknowledgements

Thank you to my close friend Maureen Smith, sister-in-law Ludivine Kadimba, colleague Mercy Chikoti and youngest daughter Evah Mwando for their support and contributions to this book.

Thanks and gratitude to all my family members who are no longer with us. Thank you to my brother Dr. Isaiah Yambeji Yikona who encouraged and initiated my interest in ophthalmic nursing.

My brother Damson Yikona and his wife Alice for their love, support and family facts, which without I would not be able to write this book.

To my family members who are too many to single out, who have supported me in life and who are one of the reasons I have written this book.

Sincere thanks are extended to all those who participated in my questionnaire.

Thank you to Kevin McKeown for financial support and advice.

Thanks to the Ministry of Health Zambia, British Council UK and the Ophthalmic Division at the Nottingham University Hospital for my development in practice and education.

Thanks to Professors Dua, Rubinstein and Amoaku for their continued support and documentation provided to students. The retired chief nurse Stephen Moss, retired Ophthalmic and IONA Vice President Joan Hamilton, Senior nurse and matron Ann Watts, Optometrist Shikha Sud and current matron Keith Knox for their overwhelming support throughout my career.

Thanks to Christine Jago for all the support, Thanks Christine, you are a true friend.

Thank you to Pastors, David Beresford, Nigel Yates and Seti Yikona, for their immense support through this book.

Thank you to Dean Murray of Eight Days a Week Print Solutions for the production of this book.

Extra special thanks to my husband Nelson, my children, Sailas, Lydia, Samonu, Evah and Mambwe for their continuing love and support.